Acknowledgements

I dedicate this book to my beloved Frankie and Uncle Bob. Their unwavering belief in me, unconditional love, and embodiment of true kindness have been a shining light for me.

Many thanks to a wonderful friend and parent, Sherri Copiak, for her proof-reading and suggestions.

As always, my husband Adison is my anchor and one-man cheering committee with his steadfast love and support.

I0159346

Forward

There are so many books on parenting out there now, far more than there were when my children were born. I had read the research, the clinical excerpts and profiles, the popular books and articles out there, but nothing prepared me for the roller-coaster ride ahead. There is no menu, there are no recipe books for success, and there is little to prepare you for the personal experience of being a parent. I loved (almost) every minute of it and take my clinical experiences of helping parents and children, as well as the personal experiences of the joy of parenting to help negotiate through and understand the developmental stages and needs of children and their parents. You are not alone! The more you know, the better in today's changing world and environment that our kids are growing up in...

Before examining the excitement and challenges, the ages and stages ahead as parents, we need to be sure you're ready as individuals and as a couple. Do you know what you're getting into? Are you prepared to turn your lives upside down?

Among the challenges of being parents together is the importance of maintaining yourselves as individuals and as a couple. Getting lost in being parents is easy, as any parent will agree. Keeping that fine balance of still being a couple apart from being parents together and of being individuals apart from being a couple needs effort, organization and fine-tuning, as there are only so many hours in a day!

Together, we will explore the demands and joys of parenthood while still being a couple who spend time together and support each other as the individuals you fell in love with...

ARE YOU READY TO BE PARENTS?

PARENTING WITH CONFIDENCE, LOVE & DIRECTION

By Dr. Karen L. Parsonson

Table of Contents

Chapter 1

The Decision to have a Child Together: Are You on the Same Page?

Having children is life-changing and there is no going back. The question is: Are you ready for it? It is not based on some biological clock, but the situation and status of your relationship that can make all the difference in the world. The decision is certainly an important one to discuss before getting together as a couple, as sometimes one party wants children and the other doesn't. This, too, can change over time. Sometimes, seeing other couple-friends having children can affect the long-term view.

We all know the data on couples who get together because of an unplanned pregnancy (supposedly 90% or more end in divorce). Making the decision together is crucial. Knowing how you both want to parent is important to discuss beforehand, as well. Some of us parent as we were parented, others parent completely differently based on their own experiences, and others parent with a combination of what they saw as working from their parents and what didn't.

There are many important things to decide beforehand, as in who is going to be the primary care-giver or is it going to be shared? How is it going to fit into both of your career plans? What are your long-term plans? How are finances going to affected and are you ready for that? What is your support system? How do your current living accommodations work for a child? How is access to schools in your neighbourhood? Are there any pre-existing health issues within either family that should be addressed before getting pregnant? Do you have good access to health care? Are you ready for the challenges ahead? These, among many others, need to be addressed.

A strong bond and good communication with each other as a couple is a primary foundation upon which to build a family. Knowing yourself and each other well is extremely important, to be able to rely upon and trust each other implicitly. Putting a career on hold is a tough decision for which there can be no regrets. Many people now decide to have children later in life, once their careers and/or advanced education are on-track with greater financial security.

The sharing of child-care responsibilities, as opposed to the more standard stay-at-home mom/working-dad seems to be the direction many people seem to be taking with the increased financial pressures of today's day-and-age. The stresses and strains many women have experienced during this transition, of working and having primary child-care and household responsibilities has created a generation of exhausted mothers trying to make a 24-hour day turn into a 48-hour day. It doesn't make for a very happy quality-of-life and surely impacts on the marital relationship. Who has time or energy to get romantic after getting home from work, having picked up the kids from a care-giver, perhaps fitting in numerous other extra-curricular activities and practices, making dinner, unpacking school bags and doing homework, the dishes, getting the kids ready for bed and their lunches made for the next day, fitting in an extra load of laundry before collapsing into bed exhausted just to start the same thing over again?

Living on one income after enjoying the benefits of two can create a more stressful financial scenario. Taking time off to raise children can cause displacement in the job-world. Missing the intellectual stimulation of co-workers and colleagues can take its toll, as well.

If parenting is to be shared, then who does what? A team approach to a pregnancy and preparation for child-birth is a good harbinger of what is to come. Even if one has babysat before, having that first child of your own is just that...a first. No amount of instruction books or parenting articles can prepare you for the first time you gaze into those trusting baby-eyes, knowing your child's very existence in that tiny body depends exclusively on you.

It is important to be sure that you are both ready and clear on what you plan to do in the future as a couple. What I'm getting at is if you are in a flurry of house-building or extended travel or career-building, having a child in that mix may not be the best time. Some goals may have to be put on hold in the short-term or indefinitely. Make sure that you both agree it's fine without any hidden resentments. They will crop up later.

Knowing you have a support system takes away some of the worry. Grand-parents, aunts and uncles, close friends and colleagues will offer lots of advice and their time. Take them up on it, as it never hurts to listen and have another perspective. But things need to be set in advance as far as "babysitting" is concerned with regards to how you have chosen to parent. One person rewarding a behaviour while another care-giver ignores or discourages it can be very confusing for children. Everyone needs to be on the same page, as much as possible. For example, if the parents are working on toilet-training but the daycare, day-home or care-giving grandparent isn't following suit, that undermines the parents' efforts. But do take those you trust up on offers to give you a break as a couple, to maintain your sanity and the adult couple bond.

Starting out life in cramped quarters can lead to greater tension and frustration. Research shows that more people living in a smaller space really does lead to greater stress. Starting out baby in a crib in your bedroom may seem great in the beginning, but where is the time for you as a couple? Where is your personal sanctuary? There needs to be room to stretch out, with a room for the child and play-space so that you're not constantly stepping on toys (although you will, even if there is a play-room, believe me!). Is your neighbourhood child-friendly, as in play-parks, green spaces? Are there other children around to socialize with?

Having schools in your neighbourhood is a bonus, as then there is no bussing or driving to school. Some future parents even choose to move to neighborhoods where there are desirable or accessible schools beforehand. School-chums will also live nearby to walk to school and home with and have play-dates. There is just no substitute for having peers from school living nearby. It's also a great way to meet other parents, potential friends for your child and for you.

Before making the decision to try for a pregnancy, you must be brutally honest with each other about any illnesses or conditions that could be passed on to your child. Sometimes, genetic counselling is an important step to allay any fears or be more realistic. It may be that taking the chance to pass on a pre-existing condition to a child is too great and adoption is something to consider. That has its own inherent difficulties and concerns, but is a wonderful option for couples who can't conceive or have severe family health issues to take into consideration.

Having good access to quality health care is critical to a healthy pregnancy and child. Attendance at health care appointments regularly during a pregnancy ensures the ongoing health of the mother and her growing baby. It is also a great bonding time for expectant fathers to hear the heart-beat for the first time, see the ultra-sound and celebrate in the growth of the couple's child together. It goes without saying that regular access to health care throughout an infant and child's life is vitally important for healthy development.

Taking all of this into account (and there are so many more questions to ask yourselves), are you sure you're ready to do this together? Do you have the unquestioning trust of each other, knowing that your partner will make the "right" decision? Do you feel respected by your partner, for who you are, all that you do? Are you being totally honest with each other about what your expectations are for being parents together? Can you communicate your feelings, your needs and wants and feel listened to? All these components of a healthy relationship and more will be stretched to the limit with your new addition…

It is a good idea to actually sit down together with a set of questions you want and need to ask each other. I'm not talking about a clinical interview here, just a relaxing opportunity to make sure that you're each certain of the other's perspective on any of the above topics we've covered. It's always better to ask than to make assumptions, because those are only guesses and you don't really know what each other thinks without asking.

Chapter 2
Timing: When is a Good Time to have a Child?

There is no "best time" to have a child. Every couple's situation is different. Some feel that having children earlier allows them to enjoy their children while they're younger while others are more inclined to wait until they feel more established in their careers, their finances and their relationships. Factors to consider are your financial situation, where you're at in your careers, the status of your relationship emotionally, physical issues, and extended family are among them. How do these all impact on your decision to have a child now or choosing to wait?

There is no question that for most couples, their earning potential grows as they mature into their careers. More seniority and experience translates into better incomes. Realistically appraising where you're both at on the income ladder and what you want to be able to give your child can help you make this decision. Will one of you stay home with the child or will you share the parental leave? More couples are sharing this special time with their child today than ever before, giving both fathers and mothers a chance to bond and enjoy this exciting new time in your lives. Have you thought through what the inevitable drop in family income will have on your lifestyle? Have you prepared in advance by saving up for the increase in expenses with a decrease in income? Be fair and do a realistic appraisal of what it will cost with your new addition...talking to new parents is a good idea, to understand all of the expenditures involved. You just might be surprised.

Where are you both at in your careers? Is it a good time to take a break from climbing up the corporate ladder? Increasingly more companies are planning for and accommodating the eventuality of their staff taking maternity time off, which is very forward-thinking. Some even have great child-care centres attached to their offices, which really takes the pressure off of their employees having to race off to a day-home or day-care at the end of the work-day. It improves the focus and productivity of their employees who don't have to worry as much about how their child is doing when they can visit with them during breaks at work.

What if one of you decides to take an extended break from work and career? How will this impact the future of your career? You have to think that with co-workers continuing to produce in the work-place, they will surpass you on the road up…are your ready for that? Is one of you ready to make a career change or re-train for a different career? Can you work out of, or study at home? Some people are able to successfully start up their own consulting businesses out of their homes while they stay home to rear their children. This can be a wonderful opportunity for them and their children, combining the best of both worlds.

If one of you has decided to stay home indefinitely, are you truly ready to leave the fast pace and energy of the corporate world? Understand that you are choosing a very different lifestyle than you're accustomed to and that may be good if you're tired of it. Remember also that you may be used to having a lot of other adults around to relate to, and try to anticipate this by making sure that you create an adult support system around you comprised of other parents in play-groups, community centres, family members or neighbours also staying home with their kids. What you don't want is to be the stereotypical stay-at-home parent waiting with baited breath for their partner to come home with news of the outside world after going stir-crazy all day with kid-talk.

I don't have to underscore the importance of being in a stable, loving relationship. That is a given. Having children to "fix" or strengthen a relationship just doesn't work, as having a child will and does create its own stresses and strains, as well. Some people see having a child as the logical next step as a couple, but are they honestly strong together, do they really know each other well enough? Certainly, we never have seen each other in every situation to be able to predict how each of us will react to something new. Take the time to listen to other couples starting a family as they talk about the upheavals and changes, as well as the thrill and joy. Really listen to your parents' stories about their early days as parents, how it changed things and how they made it work. Do you "know" each other well enough, to say that you will be able to work things through together? Have you had enough time together as a couple to feel that you are ready for this next step in your lives? You both need to be committed to the process, because there's no going back once you become parents...

Where are you both at physically? Is there an age difference between you two? Is the "biological clock" ticking and you're worried that if you wait, you may be too "old" to enjoy all the activities with your children as they grow? How do you balance out the greater energy and perhaps better heath of being younger parents with the greater maturity and perhaps stronger relationship of a couple who have been together longer? Are there health issues that you know about that may impact on pregnancy or more physical involvement in being a parent? That can have a huge impact on possibly speeding up the time-table. Health issues may also preclude you becoming pregnant or make it dangerous, so is the possibility of adoption an option? The adoption alternative, it is well-known, can be a long and arduous process, but it can give a couple that extra time to be "ready", as they anxiously wait together for the call that will change their lives and that of their "chosen child" forever.

What about extended family, how do they figure into the decision, if at all? Aging parents can speed up the time-frame for having children in order to give them and your child the wonderful opportunity of enriching each others' lives. It is a very mutual relationship, as being a grandparent and having grandparents can make such a difference in each other's lives. But this has to be figured into your overall decision carefully, as there are so many other factors to be considered: if you're not ready as a couple, if you're not ready financially, physically or emotionally, is it fair to rush things?

You may also have considered and been offered child-care help by one or both of your parents. Certainly, the younger and healthier they are, the better and longer they are going to be able to help and enjoy the grandchildren. Again, deciding on one or both of your parents as care-givers needs to be a mutual decision. Remember, any child-rearing strategies must be agreed upon, so that you are all working together. Different rules and expectations only serve to confuse a child.

Having considered and taken into account as many issues as possible, you may or may not have decided that you're ready to be parents. Listen carefully to each other's reasons and be patient…being ready together to enjoy this wonderful new stage in your life can make it all the better! In any case, reading ahead to work through child-rearing attitudes and expectations will help to set the stage for you to know each other even more…

Chapter 3
Discuss Raising your Child Together and Be Honest!

The decision to have a child is a monumental one for you as a couple. All of your hopes and dreams you have worked towards together are ready to be shared with a new dream you create together. But having a baby is one thing…how you relate to and how you raise him or her is another. If a couple hasn't talked about what their expectations are for being a parent, how they want to relate to their child, there may be some surprises!

Being a parent truly begins with conception…knowing that a life that you created together is growing inside, ready to change your lives forever. How will you both adapt and relate during the pregnancy? Will you make it a shared experience, going to doctor's appointments together and enjoying the various stages together? It's not as simple as choosing baby names…

It goes without saying that pregnancy is about eating (and drinking) for two. Whatever the mother takes in is shared with your growing baby. You really need to think about and plan for this, as your dietary habits may have to change. It goes without saying that alcohol is poison for your baby. Even one alcoholic drink of any sort at any time during a pregnancy can have disastrous effects on a child's development. It may be subtle, but why even think about taking the chance? Caffeine is another no-no, although its effects are less clear. (Remember that tea has more caffeine in it than coffee.) So, decaf it is…Drinking milk also helps promote healthy development. If you're not a great eater of vegetables, now is the time to learn to enjoy them. Together you can work together to figure out how to maintain a healthy diet. Cooking together and enjoying the same meals is a great way to get into the groove of shared family meal-times, which is so important for family communication, sharing, and bonding.

Having a birthing plan together is very important. When it comes to the actual birth, being on the same page as to procedures you want or don't want can sometimes only be advocated for by the father, as the expecting mother endures the throes of labour pains. Perhaps researching and interviewing obstetricians together as to their birthing practices can allow some fears and options to be fully understood. More specifically what I am talking about is whether you want pain medications and if so, which ones. Some prefer no medications. Others would like an epidural which, inserted through the spine, blocks sensation from that point down. There are pros and cons to each, detractors of any medication citing the research that shows more prolonged shallow breathing in newborns whose mothers have taken pain medication.

Other options to consider are episiotomies…what is the obstetrician's incidence of using them? An episiotomy is an incision made to widen and enlarge the opening of the vagina, to increase the space for the infant to emerge. There are those who prefer a natural "tear" to occur, rather than this procedure. Some maintain that an episiotomy heals more readily than a tear, others disagree. Some obstetricians will only do an episiotomy if the infant and/or mother is struggling. All of this needs to be discussed with the obstetrician in advance to alleviate as many anxieties as possible.

Then there's the issue of shaving…will the medical procedure require shaving of the pubic region? Don't laugh here…hair re-growth afterwards can be itchy! Some facilities insist on shaving, indicating that it makes the area easier to sanitize. If so, you may want to consider doing it yourself. Or you may not care in the end, because your privacy during childbirth really becomes a non-issue.

How about enemas before the birth? Any opinions on that? Many facilities insist on an enema to ensure that the increased pressure to "push" doesn't result in an early surprise on the birthing or operating table. Some also feel that full bowels can cause greater pressure on the infant making its way down and out. Yet another option to consider...

This is by no means an exhaustive list of options. There are home-births with mid-wives or doulas, water births, among many others. Who do you want in the birthing-room with you? Think about that beforehand, as what if father-to-be is at work and gets stuck in traffic on the way to the hospital? Whoever is going to be there has to help maintain as calm and relaxing an environment as possible. Remember, no birth is picture-perfect from what a couple envisions! Being together on a birthing plan can help share the burden, giving the mother some peace-of-mind when it comes down to the actual birth.

Then, there are the considerations of whether you want rooming-in after the birth. Depending upon how long mother and baby remain in hospital after the birth (and it is far shorter than it was years ago), the infant can remain in the room with the mother and family for easy feedings and family bonding. The advantages of this include, of course, early bonding but also practice in breast-feeding. Another option to discuss is whether the infant is to be breast-fed. If the infant remains in the maternity nursery, they will be fed with a sugar-water solution when they are hungry. Some see the advantage of not rooming-in so that the recovering mother can rest and recover after the birth.

The literature is filled with information on the benefits of breast-milk for varying lengths of time. Most advocate for at least the first three months, to ensure that the infant receives the necessary antibodies and protection from the mother's body. At the beginning, colostrum is produced by the mother, not the fat-enriched milk. It is the colostrum that carries the mother's antibodies to pass on to the infant. If breast-feeding is the option that you choose, then you should consider how the father can participate, as he doesn't have the necessary equipment to breast-feed! Sharing in feedings by expressing breast-milk to be fed by bottle is an option, but understand that for most infants, it is easier to suckle on a breast than a nipple from a bottle. Once the infant can feed from a bottle, sometimes they don't want to go back to the breast. There is obviously a lot to consider here!

Will you have some help when Mom and baby come home from the hospital? Will one of your Moms come over to give her some rest and respite? Maybe some other extended family or friends are willing to help? This can be really helpful if your relationships with in-laws are good ones and the length of time they stay is discussed and agreed-upon in advance.

What about diapers? Every infant needs them. Will you use disposables or cloth diapers? There are some amazing cloth diapers out there on the market today. If you choose the cloth option, will you have a diaper service or do the job at home? If it's at home, is it going to be a shared responsibility? As much laundry as an infant generates from clothing changes alone, that amount increases incrementally with keeping up with diapers.

Now, we look at how you hope to share the responsibility once mother and infant are back home. Will the infant share the family bed? Will you put a cradle or bassinette in your room? Will you put the crib in your room? Will you have a crib in the infant's nursery nearby? Who will do late-night feedings? Will you share the responsibility, so each of you gets a chance to get more sleep? Be prepared for a lot less sleep, whatever way you look at it...

What about child-care, is one or both of you staying home for any length of time? Is extended family going to provide any child-care? How will you work things out with ensuring you both get as much rest as possible? Are you willing to divide up responsibilities at home, like meals, laundry, bill-paying or house-keeping?

When it comes to feeding, what are your personal dietary choices? Are you vegetarian? If so, you will no doubt choose to raise your children with the same dietary choices. How will you work together to meet your child's dietary needs, with their greater requirements for protein? If you're organic, no doubt you'll continue the same for your children. If you really dislike veggies, how will you ensure that your children can acquire a taste for and enjoy vegetables? Is one or are both of you lactose-intolerant or do you have a strong allergy to some foods? You need to figure that into the equation as a possibility for your child.

Now that we've looked at questions to ask yourselves about the physical, work and time issues, have you talked about parenting strategies? Remember that rules and/or discipline (not a negative term!) should be mutually agreed upon. If one parent sets one bedtime and the other doesn't follow through, if one encourages bedtime snacks and the other discourages them, it can be very confusing for a child. As nit-picky as this may seem, the more you have figured out beforehand, the easier it will be to follow through and enforce things together.

What about rewards? What about consequences? Are you agreed to be as encouraging as possible, noting every little positive you can and giving your child strokes for their attempts? (Much more on positive reinforcement and building your child's self-confidence later.) Have you talked about what age-appropriate consequences you can both agree to? Here, I'm talking about disciplinary actions: withdrawal of privileges, loss of favourite items, time-outs, among others. Whatever you've agreed upon as far as rewards and consequences are concerned, **follow through**. I can't stress this enough, as broken promises (for rewards) and idle threats (of consequences) are what children will remember.

If children don't believe you when you say they'll be rewarded for doing something right or disciplined for doing something wrong, you have lost any leverage (as well as their respect, as it means you're not as good as your word). Eventually, they should be self-motivated to do the right thing and do it well as they mature, but when they are younger, their behaviour needs to be guided. Similarly, developing a conscience (as in knowing not to do the wrong thing) is something that doesn't necessarily come naturally or make sense to them, so children need to learn it from parents.

Remember that children make note of which parent is "softer" and easier to potentially get a "yes" answer from and will seek that parent out. Playing good cop/bad cop with kids doesn't win you any favours and can develop a wedge between you. Consistency in a home is much more straightforward and predictable for a child and for each other. **Never** disagree on the actions either of you is taking in front of a child (unless, of course, those actions are abusive). *Always present a united front.* You are a team and let them see that so they can become a part of the team.

It may feel like I'm getting ahead of things, but do you have you considered schools? Amazing as it may seem with the competitiveness of today's world, many parents pre-register their children in pre-schools, elementary schools which lead into their preferred high schools in the future. Do you live in the catchment area for the school you want or will you have to move? Does it matter because you want him or her to go to a private school? What about extra-curricular activities? Of course, they will depend upon the individual child as to what they are suited to, but are there things you would like to able to share with your child in activities you enjoy?

This is by no means an exhaustive list, because there are so many issues in raising children that they can catch you off-guard. What I'm suggesting is talking through as many of your personal choices, your own personal experiences, attitudes and beliefs as possible to lay your cards on the table. I'll discuss more specific issues that arise at each age-level as we progress though each stage.

Chapter 4

Pregnancy as a Couple: Doing it Together

I find it adorable and enchanting to hear a couple celebrating that: "we're pregnant!". We all know how it used to be…pregnancy was a mystery that women went through with each other's support and dads waited out in the waiting room walking circles in the carpet awaiting the news. No more. It's wonderful to see couples attending medical appointments together, in birthing classes together, looking through pregnancy books together, planning and decorating nurseries together, both sharing in the experience.

Pregnancy is less of a mystery today than ever before, as people are better informed about the various stages and health issues. No longer do they rely only on their family doctor to monitor their progress. They are aware of possible concerns and complications, maternal diet and health, the impact of alcohol and cigarettes on the developing foetus and more of what to expect as the pregnancy progresses. Regular doctor's appointments and birthing classes keep them up with the latest information.

Attending appointments and hearing the heart-beat for the first time is an event that marks the beginning for many couples of truly realizing that they have created a new life together. Reading about it is one thing, but experiencing the sound of those heartbeats, hearing them together, is a moment never to be forgotten. The same goes for that first ultrasound at around 16 weeks…to see that little person growing inside is a life-changing event.

Depending upon where you live, some states and provinces have birthing classes through community health programs. Others require you to seek them out. In any case, attending them together, learning with other couples about how the big event will proceed and how to work together is really a wonderful experience that draws you even closer. Knowing that your partner knows what is happening and how to help with breathing exercises and massage is a big relief for a pregnant first-time mom. It's a sharing of responsibility and knowledge that you can back each other up when you need it.

I always believe that knowledge is power and the more we can understand something it advance, the better we're prepared. All that being said, there are some wonderful books out there specific to the various stages of pregnancy, infancy and early childhood development. I remember myself the excitement of reading through the books, tracing my progress in each pregnancy and the development of the babies. Sharing the excitement with their father, looking at the pictures together and imagining the size of the foetus at each stage became a glorious shared experience. It also helps for a young father to read and fully understand what is happening with and within the body of the mother of his child…that her body will never be the same again and what it takes to go through pregnancy.

Whether you choose to find out the gender from your first ultrasound (or if they can even tell for sure), making up the nursery together makes it feel even more real in the excitement of preparing the baby's room. Painting (remember, use only low VOC paints and limit mother-to-be's exposure to it!), wall-papering, buying or borrowing the crib (remember, regulations for cribs change over time! Ensure that it still meets today's safety standards!!!), buying the layette and those first tiny clothes and diapers, the infant car-seat (the same goes for them, the regulations change over time!), the stroller, baby monitor, bibs…so many things you've never bought before! You'll learn about it all together as you research out products and prices, creating a beautiful room that will be safe and ready for your newborn to come home to.

You may choose to change some of your eating habits together, ensuring the best possible nutrition for the developing foetus.

You may even (if you don't already) cook together working towards a healthier lifestyle. Depending upon how tired pregnant mom is, you may or may not have as active a social life. Keeping up with friends as a couple maintains a great cheering committee and support group for both of you. Some may even be going through or have gone through the same life change and that really helps, seeing how they're coping. They can help you alleviate any fears and worries, sharing their experiences and ideas.

There are numerous books written out there about sex and pregnancy and I'll just touch on some of the issues: changes in sex drive during the stages of pregnancy, the safety of sex during a pregnancy, and being open to different approaches. First off, everyone is different in how their bodies respond to what may be the same experience. I had read about pregnant women having a particularly high sex drive during the second trimester (the 4th to 6th month of pregnancy) and it being significantly reduced in the last (7th to 9th month). Having spoken to many women (it's a shared experience we seem to like to describe to each other) about the pregnancy and births of their children, I have heard sometimes very conflicting views from their experience. Some felt no difference throughout the pregnancy or it was different between pregnancies, some felt as great a drive throughout and some lost their drive altogether. Some said it changed through the stages of their pregnancies. It depends upon the person and the couple, how they adapt and communicate, as well.

Communication is the key between sexual partners (just as in any stage of a relationship) as to how they're feeling, what feels good or could feel better. It's also important to focus on fathers, as well. Their love isn't any less for the mother of their future child, yet they may have fears of the impact intercourse can have on the developing foetus. That may be a shared concern between both partners. Sex and intercourse can be enjoyed through all stages of pregnancy physically without risk to the foetus. Of course, if it is a high-risk pregnancy, there may be some concerns that your doctor may share with you about anything strenuous or too physical and this may preclude intercourse. Some fathers are afraid to "hurt" their pregnant mates and again, sharing these fears with each other is something you can work through together.

I can't underscore here how important it is to **listen** to each other...don't make assumptions, ask. Don't harbour resentments, ask and be clear. Some pregnant moms don't feel they are seen as attractive or sexually appealing and if that is the case, a nervous father may give the wrong message when they want nothing more than to be sexual, finding their wife's changing body beautiful and sexy. As we've seen in the tabloids and magazines, the physical changes to a woman's body during pregnancy are beautiful and to be celebrated, not hidden.

So maybe you need to adapt to body changes in what feels good for both of you...sex during pregnancy can create new and excitingly different alternatives to explore. Try out new positions that work for both of you. And if intercourse becomes uncomfortable or not as pleasurable, remember that there is so much more to sex than intercourse alone and that's okay. Maintaining the feelings of intimacy and closeness as a couple are what are most important. Cuddling alone is a wonderful shared feeling of intimacy.

Let's get more specific about body changes and sensitivities during pregnancy. Surely the most obvious change is a growing tummy...hence the need for maternity clothes for most as they progress through the stages. Seeing your tummy grow and tracking the size of the growing foetus is exciting, but can bring up worries and anxieties the closer you get to the birth...how is that baby going to actually make it out? It seems impossible and that's one of the amazing things about life, but we've all made it out of there, one way or another!

Breasts grow and become more tender, hips may begin to grow and/or spread, changes may happen in facial skin (remember, hormones are changing), the added weight may make feet swell, appetite and food preferences may change, the body's biochemistry may change (some women become diabetic or pre-diabetic), some women experience changes in their hair texture, the body may retain water, sleeping may be more difficult and require some adjustments with pillows and position to be comfortable. Not everyone experiences all of these changes, but remember that a pregnant body is literally adjusting to nurture two...mother and growing baby. How can there not be changes?

Living in a body that is literally not your own (as you knew it) anymore can be exciting, wondrous and thrilling, but at the same time a lot to take in. So many changes all at once (even if gradual and expected) can be overwhelming. Talking with other women who have given birth gives reassurance about changes, that things will return to "normal" again physically, each in our own time. The more that your partner understands about what you're going through, the better they can appreciate, be supportive and share in every stage.

With the hormonal and body changes of pregnancy come the emotional changes and mood swings. A pregnant woman is, after all, a woman who has already experienced the hormonal peaks and valleys of the infamous menstrual cycle. At least that's somewhat predictable for most, but there is no cycle of what to predict during a pregnancy. It is a totally new experience and again is experienced differently by every woman. She can be extremely sensitive, laugh one minute and cry the next. She may not feel in control of her emotions or her body at all and that can be a scary experience for anyone, let alone a spouse who has no idea what is happening.

Be patient with yourself, be patient with each other. This is a new experience for you both. Listen to how each of you is feeling. Don't focus on behaviours and assume you know what they mean. Focus on going through this together and supporting each other. The end goal is something beautiful together. When you've survived the experience and look back, you'll realize how hard you worked together to achieve a wonderful dream: a child together. Then, the new challenges begin!

Chapter 5
Nurturing from within and the infant parent-bond: Early connections

Just as you're learning to relate to each other differently, you're also establishing a connection, a bond to your developing baby. A mother can feel that first flutter like a butterfly stirring inside her. Not so for a father. The first he can begin to really feel is the first kicks, the baby's movements within the mother. Sharing in the doctor's visits together helps both fathers-to-be and mothers-to-be in experiencing the signs of development: the first time they hear the heart-beat, that first glimpse of their growing child together in the ultra-sound.

While fathers can't experience the same physical reminders of the growing infant from within, they can share in the same connections a mother starts to establish with the baby growing inside her. She no-doubt begins to start talking to her growing tummy, sharing her day and responding to the kicks and flutters. Some pregnant moms even sing to their growing baby, getting ready for the lullabies to help coo them to sleep at night.

Research has shown that the first sounds newborns recognize are the voices they have heard while cuddled in the warmth of the womb. Most often, it is the mother's voice that they have heard most frequently and closely, reverberating inside. For dads to feel closer to their growing child, it makes natural sense that they do what moms have done forever: talk to the growing child within. Knowing what we do about voice-recognition after birth, wouldn't it make sense for dads to talk to, sing to, even read stories to their baby-to-be? Sharing the closeness and intimacy of that experience as a couple can also only help to bring the two parents closer.

People, even strangers, are notorious for thinking that a pregnant woman's tummy is out there for them to rub or touch. It's not an open invitation. Projecting "out there" is enough to make a woman feel a spectacle, never mind sometimes unwelcome pats or rubs, like the "cheek-pinching" of cute little kids by their elders. But the intimacy, the sharing of their growing baby makes for wonderful, cuddling intimate moments for the couple. This physical connection of two people who created the growing life together serves to bring them even closer.

All this talk about "closeness" and "sharing" may seem trite. Of course the couple got "close", they made a baby together! And when it comes down to it, all that a pregnant woman can "share" is what her partner can feel and admire from the outside, not the physical changes and discomforts happening within. But talking about it, encouraging the rubs, the pats, the chats to Junior, makes it a shared experience. There is no greater wonder that a couple can experience together to affirm their love.

As already mentioned, talking about your plans together for the baby only serves to make everything a shared experience. The closer and more connected the couple, the warmer and more supportive an environment for the newborn to snuggle into outside of the safety of their nest inside. Just as babies have been shown to respond inside to biological input (as in cigarette smoking increases their heart-rate), they also respond to the emotional tone or responses of the mother. Increased tension, stress or anxiety is experienced as the same by the baby. It only makes sense that feelings of calm, relaxation and harmony would impact more positively on the baby within. Parents who create and maintain a supportive, harmonious and happy relationship can only help to induce the same for their growing baby, both inside and out.

To the dads experiencing perhaps alarming or unusual changes in your mate's diet or preferences (who hasn't heard of cravings for pickles and ice cream?), revel in the experience. Indulge together in the wackiness of the moment. Rub her sore back, massage her tired feet, prepare (and maybe even share in) warm baths. If she's taking a nap, cuddle in together. There won't be many of these peaceful moments ahead for a little while, at least. Create memories of this time together to look back on and smile.

The stronger the connection between the couple about-to-be-parents, the greater they will be able to withstand the give-and-take of the unexpected when they become a family of 3. After all, they can prepare as much as possible, but no one can be totally ready for the changes and surprises ahead.

Chapter 6

Birth & the Home-coming

You have the bags packed, your birthing lessons under your belt, the nursery ready, the infant car-seat ready, your birthing plans figured out, and now you're waiting for it all to begin…the count-down to the 40th week has been ongoing. Maybe you've had a false-start or two, the early contractions of Braxton Hicks preparing the body for the real thing.

Maybe things haven't been going as planned, the birth earlier than expected, having to be induced or by an unexpected C-section, maybe baby is way overdue. Remember, few (if any!) births are as picture perfect as you imagined.

What you do have is each other, through it all. Having a solid birthing plan can go awry when the unexpected happens, but following through as much as possible with partners advocating for their mate goes a long way to creating an enduring, positive memory. With a woman in the throes of labour pains, it can be very hard for her to see all that is going on. Her partner becomes her eyes and ears to the flurry of activity. The more anyone knows about what's going on, the more they can feel in control of an uncontrollable situation. Talk to her, walk with her if she can to help the forces of gravity move things along. Ask the doctors and nurses if she can suck on some ice. Hold her hand, rub her back, ask the questions she wants answered. Allow her to focus as much as she can comfortably on a safe delivery for herself and the baby. If you can, let family members know what's going on but don't leave her if she says she needs you.

How long will it all take? Some lucky women have gone through labor and delivery in a few short hours. Others may take much, much longer. My first child was a 30-hour ordeal, while my second was 17 hours (from when the first real contractions began). You can't rush it for it to be safe for mother and baby.

Every woman's birthing experience will be different and will probably be different for each labor and delivery for each woman.

As much as it is an exciting experience, it can be a scary one, too. All of the technology, and the non-stop nurses and doctors coming and going can make for much confusion. What if your doctor can't make it in time or is unexpectedly away? That's when your partner can step up to get everyone on the same page the best he or she can. If plans are changed because complications arise, ask questions but realize that these people have done this many times before. You can only do as much as you can do. If an unplanned c-section has to be done to ensure the health and safety of mom and baby, so be it. That is the end goal: a safe arrival of a healthy baby and a healthy mom.

Once you hear that first cry, see that pink little body and red face, it will all have been worth it. Surprises can occur during the birth with some babies struggling and needing extra attention. We have all heard about and fear it, but let the medical personnel do what they need to do. They know what has to be done and will let you know as soon as they've done their job and your baby is ready for your introduction and attention. As soon as mother can hold her baby and father gets his chance, everything will feel alright again.

Let's not forget that while baby is getting his or her attention, mom is still struggling with the after-birth involving labour pains again. She still needs to be monitored very closely for what her body is going through. It is not a done-deal once she has given birth. She may have torn during delivery or needed an episiotomy, both of which require stitching-up. She may be haemorrhaging, requiring IVs and extra medical attention but her focus is on baby. Medical personnel know that the soonest it is physically possible for newborn and mom to reconnect, the better. Still, it depends upon the medical attention that each requires.

What if baby must receive more intensive medical attention before he or she can be held? Let's appreciate that this is a scary situation for both parents. The more they can be supportive of each other, the better. The more information they can receive about baby's condition, the better they can understand and prepare. It may be up to dad to find out more while mom is receiving her further medical attention, but he has to find out for both of them. Understand and appreciate that medical personnel are prepared for every possibility and will do their best to let you know what is happening.

Every facility is different in its policies and procedures as in how soon or for how long parents can hold and connect with their newborn. Giving both parents a chance to recover from the birth, mothers physically and emotionally drained and fathers riding on adrenalin also gives baby a chance to adjust away from all the clamour.

I am always so sad for an infant at birth and at the beginning of their time out in the world. As wonderful as it is for parents and family to experience the joy of their arrival, I can't help but think of how confusing and stressful it must be coming out into the world for the first time. It was really quiet and dark inside floating around in the safety of their mother's womb and out they come into the harsh light, bombarded by noises and people, every sense taxed to the maximum. Birth is generally not a gentle process for mom or baby. Some try to make accommodations with choosing water births or silent births or muted lights in birthing rooms that are less technical in appearance, but at the end of the day, being tugged or pushed out into the harsh world of reality can't help but be a traumatic experience.

As soon as possible, now no-longer-pregnant mom can be moved to her hospital room. I can't underscore what a strange feeling it is for the first time after baby is out in the world to not feel him or her inside you. It feels so foreign to not have the closeness of the heart-beat, of the flutters, kicks and "swooshes" inside. As thrilling as it was to finally see that wonderful little person who was growing inside you, there can be an almost yearning for the wonder of how that felt. It takes a while to adjust to not being a "twosome" anymore.

We've talked about "rooming-in" or the baby staying in the hospital nursery as mom recovers and it may not be for long, as many women are now returning home the day after the birth. Of course, everything depends upon the physical condition and recovery of mom and baby.

What if baby must stay in the hospital for a little while? Maybe he or she came early and needs to be in an incubator for a bit. It's not the ideal, picture-perfect story of going home with baby, but you can both keep as close as possible with visits, holding them or being able to touch them gently as their condition permits. It is certainly much harder not being able to bring your baby home with you and I can't underscore how traumatic it can be. Again, being together for each other at this time is crucial, supporting and listening to each other.

When it is time to bring baby home, whether with you or afterwards, it is the beginning of a wonderful new life together. As you pack up all of your things and that adorable little bundle to take out to the car for the first time, you realize it's all up to you both now. Gazing into those trusting little baby eyes, knowing that your child's life is in your hands in every respect is an awe-inspiring moment. Driving to your baby's new home for the first time, having checked and double-checked and triple-checked that the car-seat is installed properly, you're going home together for the first time. A new little family has begun on its journey together…

Chapter 7

Creating a Life around your New Little Family

Having made it home together safely after your first of many car rides together, you bring your baby to his or her new home. There may be family waiting to help you out during these first few days or weeks. That is wonderful and appreciated support, but at the same time, you're probably wanting to create your own routines and sense of family. By all means, realize that helpers are there to get you some rest and ease in the transition. Take whatever rest you can because it can be a lot to handle on your own all at once. At the same time, take comfort in knowing that they do not expect you to treat them as guests. They are there to help, not create more work for you. If they've made meals for you, that's great. If they can help out with baby-laundry or cleaning, that's great too but you know what routines you want to set in place for your family. Now is the time to set them in place.

Everyone has an opinion about and their own way of raising their children. People are even more opinionated about babies, sometimes expecting first-time parents to not know anything. You may not have the experience yet, but times and practices change over time. The way babies are supposed to sleep, how much you put in their crib with them, what types of bottles or diapers to use, whether to breast-feed or not, whether to feed-on-demand or not, how to burp them best have all been debated and changed as to what is considered the best and safest practice over the years.

You've taken the pre-natal courses, some of you have babysat, and/or you may have friends or family who have recently given birth. There are so many sources of information available and you've hopefully talked about and decided how you want to do things. What may have worked for others before surely did work for them, but there is always new information and updates with new ideas. You will learn and figure out what works best for you and your baby. You took the time to research and discuss how you want to do things, so follow it if it works for you.

There is no doubt that age-old "tricks of the trade" in terms of burping or rocking or swaddling an infant have proven their mettle. You should try things your own way, as well. Everyone develops confidence from trying and succeeding. Inexperience leaves people lacking in confidence, but every attempt will help you feel better that you can take care of your baby.

Support each other in your attempts. I think all of us have heard fathers being castigated for not doing diaper-duty enough, while they bemoan the fact that early-on they were told they weren't "doing it right" and gave up. No one is an expert at the beginning with their own baby. What works for one may not work for another. If someone is trying, give him or her some positive feedback for their efforts.

Remember that each baby is different. Some may cry incessantly during a diaper change because they're cold (keep something nearby to cover up their chest and tummy while changing them, making sure it doesn't cover their face). Others don't seem to care. Some babies burp beautifully the traditional way from being held upright and patting their backs, others seem to respond best to lying on their tummies and having their backs rubbed to a resounding belch. Some seem to sleep all the time, others seem to like more stimulation and attention, staying awake longer. No two babies are alike, as parents of a second child will often be heard saying how different their second child is to their first.

If you have any concerns or worries, always ask. If your concerns persist, see your doctor. Never leave any worry aside. Nervous first-time parents may be just that, but isn't it better to be safe than sorry? There is no stupid question when it comes to your baby's health and welfare.

Creating your own little routines as you struggle to figure out your baby's schedule is always a challenge at the beginning. The goal for many parents to get some sleep is that first night when baby slept through the night. Taking turns in the meantime to wake up and bring baby for a feeding really helps and in the future, that team spirit is warmly remembered.

Just as I explained that a baby's first sound recognition is often of the mother's voice (hence I suggested that dads get in on the pregnancy chatter), facial recognition is also pre-wired to a focal point from the mother's breast to her face. In other words, they can see best at the distance from breast-feeding to the mother's face as she feeds them. Again, this can require some adjustments for dads to be seen and recognized. Try and make those feedings a "family affair", not just mother and baby. The more baby and dad can interact, see each other and feel close, the faster and more comfortable their bond will be.

Try and involve baby in your regular couple routines like making dinner, doing dishes or eating together if he or she is awake. Snuggled in a baby sling like a Snuggee close to you or cradled in an infant seat, they can get used to the sounds of the family and you can enjoy their reactions and sounds. The more you become a part of each others' lives, the more natural it will feel. A word of caution here: never (I mean never!) leave a baby unattended in a carrier on any elevated surface. All it takes is just one untoward movement to possibly cause a tumble to the floor.

What if baby is "colicky" or you have problems getting him or her to sleep? That can create two cantankerous parents sleep-walking on the edge of exhaustion! Talking to other family members and friends who are parents about what worked for them, whether incessant rocking, the sound of the vacuum cleaner, the vibration of the dryer, going for drives may have worked for them. If everything you've tried hasn't worked, a trip to the doctor may be in order, as the misery a constantly crying baby must be feeling is not something to be ignored. It's the only way they can express themselves. Many times, it has been found that the infant is experiencing terrible stomach pains but can't really tell anyone in any other way than to cry (in pain). It's far better to know the possible cause of the crying than to wait it out. Remember, your baby is trusting you to help and has no other way to tell you.

Trust yourselves that you will learn the meaning of every sound your baby makes over time...the cry of hunger, of a wet diaper, of a need for a cuddle, of boredom and a need for attention. It is their language and way to express their needs. You will eventually learn it, it just takes time.

The best advice at this time is to become a team. Learn your baby's "lingo", be responsive to your partner's exhaustion or frustration. Take care of each other. If someone needs a break, give him or her time for a quiet bath, a nap or a walk. Be patient with each other and this will be a time you remember together with fondness...when you pulled together and became a little family.

Chapter 8

The early months: Growth & nurturance

You've survived those first few days at home and are beginning to figure out what your baby needs and wants from their cries. You're getting into some sort of pattern or groove (albeit still unpredictable) and have some sense of normalcy developing. At this stage, you're marking your days by the frequency of feedings, how long you may be able to sleep in-between night-time feedings, the frequency of diaper changes needed, how much laundry you have to do, your baby's growth and ability to focus. You count their life on earth by days.

You note every movement of those tiny fingers and toes. You watch their little eyes as they gaze and start to focus more on their surroundings. You listen attentively to their vocalizations: cries, coos, gurgles, burps, diaper sounds. You beam with pride after the doctors' appointments that show they're growing by weight and length. You proudly start to go on outings in the stroller or by car, marvelling at showing your world to your baby and your baby to the world.

Now is the time to start filling in those baby books you may have gotten as a present at your baby shower. If you didn't get one, buy one or make a scrap-book, yourself. These exciting memories will fade with time, replaced by new ones with the rapid development that happens in these early days and months. Every memory is a treasure to be kept.

Some of your mobility may be constrained by the climate where you live. Coming from a sometimes very cold winter climate myself, depending upon what season your baby is born, walks in strollers may be tough out of concern for keeping baby warm. The same can be said of drives...the transitions from a warm home to the car and the car to your destination can be worrisome.

Of course, you know that bundling up is the way to go. Getting outside of the house is important for baby to see what's out there and for parents to get out into the world again.

Your growing baby's strength starts developing from head and neck down. So does their ability to see and respond to more around them. With their neck being able to hold up their head more, they can start to see things from a different vantage point. Their eyes strengthen and they can start to focus on objects farther away. They can begin to move their head to look around and try to find the sources of sounds that they hear. I can remember the first time my then-baby brother, carried by my Dad, became fascinated by the sound of dripping water from a faucet. Dad cradled him by the faucet and his little head turned to watch it drip, his little body wriggling in excitement. Every sound is new to them, every sight and color a marvel. Re-experiencing the world through your baby's eyes and ears is an amazing experience.

At first, it appears babies respond to contrasts in colors…whether black and white or otherwise. They tend to focus on the borders where colors meet. Movement, too, catches their attention and crib mobiles can provide hours of enjoyment. Responding to your baby's attention, movements and recognition with talking and attention allows them to start to understand their world around them. Just because they can't speak for you to understand them doesn't mean they aren't starting to understand you. A child can understand far more than 100 times what they can express, as you will learn when they start to talk.

I am a firm believer in stimulating your child's growing senses, learning, and movements from the beginning. A proviso here: over-stimulation or bombarding them with too much at once can be overwhelming. Music has been shown to aid development and it certainly can have a calming effect, as we have learned from singing them lullabies. I fondly remember rocking and singing Louis Armstrong's "What a Wonderful World" to my baby daughter for hours to get her to sleep at night. She still responds to that song with a smile even as an adult, somehow the association perhaps twigging a distant fond memory.

Talking to your baby, helping them associate names and words for what is around them helps them to understand more and more over time. Think of yourself as a narrator of a story, the play-by-play of your day, and chat as you go along. It may feel like you're talking to yourself (and that's okay!), but you're not. You have a captive audience there of your little one paying rapt attention to your every word. Who else would be so appreciative of our nattering all day long? One thing's for sure…you're never alone when you have a baby in the house!

Infant massage, a rapidly-growing practice, is soothing for baby and a wonderful way to maintain that physical connection with your baby. There are some wonderful classes out there for parents and babies to learn to connect this way. Even before this became a popular practice, both of my children loved being stroked rhythmically as babies, stretching, gurgling and squealing in pleasure. Whether it's while you're changing their diaper, getting them ready for bed or in the bath, infant massage is a gentle and soothing physical connection with your baby.

Just like massage is a wonderful way to comfort and connect with your baby, bath-time can be a joy. Some babies don't like being naked and it can make bathing a struggle, but the warmth of the water can be a temptation they learn to love. The frequency of baby baths recommended nowadays is less than when we were young, with concerns for drying out baby's skin, removing naturally-occurring skin oils. A huge variety of bathing products is now available to keep baby's skin healthy. That notwithstanding, the pleasure of sharing in watching your baby squeal and giggle in the water can be a joyous experience for couples to share. One caveat: many babies really don't like water on their heads and faces. However, that is the only way to shampoo them. Humming and singing to them as you do it can often be soothing. Remember that you mustn't get water into their ears, as they are a breeding-ground for infections. As an adult, I still can remember how painful earaches were as a child. Again, your baby can't tell you what hurts, only that something is bothering them. More about ear infections later...

As baby can move more, he or she begins to focus on their fingers and toes, a wonderful pastime and form of amusement. They don't know yet that they're part of them, so it's like having built-in toys! Every gain in mobility gives a baby the opportunity to experience more of their world. I can remember like it was yesterday when both of my children could roll over on their own for the first time. They had been trying to for awhile, but suddenly with the blink of an eye, they had done it and could see things from a whole new perspective. What an amazing feeling of freedom and success for them!

I have never been a proponent of babies spending too much time (other than sleeping) in their cribs. Granted, babies do need to learn how to comfort and amuse themselves without parents always being at their beck-and-call, but keeping them around you in a stroller, a Snuggee or an infant seat keeps them in on the action so they can enjoy the pleasure of your company and you theirs. Humans are social creatures and encouraging that interaction from an early age helps prepare them for more in the future.

I am not a fan of babies and television. Yes, there are colors and sounds and stimulation abounds, but it is passive. They just watch it go by with no feedback, no human interaction. Television is not and should never be a babysitter. It can provide background music or sound, but as a primary source of attention, it fails miserably.

Remember that babies can and will "make strange" with people they are not familiar with. It's not personal. They're just creatures of habit and feel more comfortable around and with people they are used to. Sometimes, it can even happen with one or the other parent. Babies and children will reverse loyalties at times, preferring to be comforted, fed or changed by one parent rather than the other. It has nothing to do with the other parent's ability to comfort them, so again, don't take it personally.

As babies develops their senses, verbalizations and movements, encourage them and respond with your own excitement at every new development. Tempt them with new sounds and sights, revelling in the joy of their reactions. Celebrate each new step in their ability to move themselves, gaining more control over their bodies and their environment. Don't, however, push them. Everyone develops at her or his own pace. If they can't hold their head up on their own yet, wait until their necks are strong enough. That little head can be pretty heavy for them to hold up! Don't push it!!! You may be following their progress according to what the baby books say is "normal", but understand what is normal for one may not be for another. Again (and I will continue to repeat this over and over), if you have concerns about your baby's development, ask your doctor to allay any fears. The sooner any developmental issues are caught, the sooner they can be understood and receive intervention.

Chapter 9

Development through the 1ˢᵗ year

You're probably counting your baby's age in months, not days now. You've come to know and understand your baby better, their likes and dislikes, how they express themselves, all of their little "quirks" up to this point. Following along the natural development and strengthening of senses and muscle-tone, baby has achieved the mile-stones of holding their head up, turning their head to sounds and sights, rolling over for the first time and now as they like it, reaching for and playing with hands and toes. From their new vantage point, they can experience new and varied sights and sounds and are starting to respond to them with varying sounds, themselves. You are now able to experience the world through their eyes.

The first year of life marks the greatest leaps of development for a human being. From its first breaths, helpless and totally dependent, during that first year an infant can use and process all of its senses, vocalize to express itself, and has gained control over much of its muscles and body. Think of how far your baby has come!

On first entering this world, a baby's senses are still used to the relatively quiet and darker world inside the womb. The light, colors and intensity of sounds outside are confusing at first and baby is pre-wired to recognize voices it heard from within, as well as the visual focal length from their face at the breast to a mother's face gazing down at them. As their eye muscles strengthen, they can begin to focus at greater distances and direct their eyes around. Familiar faces and places begin to be recognized with experience. The same goes for sounds: the association of voices with people they come to expect from hearing them, the noises in a home around them they come to experience and recognize. Their sense of touch helps them to begin making associations as they gain control over their hands and fingers, reaching out to touch things around them. Taste and smell, so closely associated, are stimulated as they begin the journey through pablum to solid foods, developing their own taste preferences.

From being cradled and viewing the world only in a lying position, your baby learns to move its head and neck, then its hands to start to reach for and grasp things, to roll over and see the world right-side-up. That in itself: moving on demand, is a huge difference. Having the muscle strength and tone to sit up (whether supported at first, then on their own) gives them an even greater view of and ability to interact with the world. Next on the physical development agenda, starting to creep and then crawl, using their legs and feet starts to give them greater mobility and access to the world around them. With greater leg strength and arm strength to help pull them up, standing and then surfing and walking around things to hold onto gives even greater freedom to move around.

From those first cries upon coming into the world, baby starts to make clear to others their need and wants. They learn that to get someone's attention, they need to express themselves, which they do on a regular basis! Their cries become more varied as parents learn to respond to what different-sounding cries mean. In the beginning, every parent is confused as they try to figure out if a diaper is wet, if baby is hungry, if they're bored or lonely, wanting some attention or feeling discomfort. With greater vocal control, babies begin to gurgle and coo, babble and laugh…who can't remember the first time they heard their little one chortle or giggle? Isn't it just the most amazing, remarkable, joyous event? As baby's vocalizations begin to sound more like syllables and recognizable words or names, we listen for that first one we can associate with ourselves. Be honest with yourselves…who isn't waiting for "mama" or "dada" to come out? The sounds may or may not really mean anything we would understand, but baby is learning to make associations of sounds with people and things. A cardinal rule is that they understand far more that they hear than they can express. In other words, what they say may not yet be intelligible, but they understand more and more each day.

Make feeding time a fun time, eating together if you can. Exploring new tastes and sensations of each new food you introduce is an experience to be shared! Following the feeding plans of experts, working your way through veggies and fruits, watching your baby's face as they try something new is a marvel to behold. From those first foods you feed them to finger-foods they can jam into their own mouths, now the fun begins. Who would want to miss that?

With each physical and sensory leap in development, the baby's brain is developing leaps and bounds. They are starting to make sense of their world. They are interacting with it more and more. They are expressing themselves, learning associations, how things work with the people and things in their lives. They have become more of a part of it, able to do things and reach out. Their brains, bodies and senses are ready for everything they see and hear. They're like little sponges for every sight, sound, and touch.

When we hear other parents and family talking about their children's stages of development, we can't help but make comparisons. Someone's baby was walking by 10 months, someone's baby said its first word at 9 months. This one rolled at 3 months, that one crawled at 5 months. Remember, <u>every child is different and will develop at his or her own pace and in their own way</u>. Try not to fret or compare. Some babies develop faster verbally or physically than others and development is rarely, if ever, even. There are huge leaps and bounds that cannot be predicted.

Physically, some little ones skip over crawling altogether and begin walking, missing a "milestone". Some quiet babies don't do much babbling, but start chatting with you and/or themselves unexpectedly. Some may appear to be totally disinterested in the sounds around them, but focus intently on the chatter around them. Pay attention to their attempts and give them verbal feedback as much as you can. Let them know you're watching and listening.

Let's look at ways to help stimulate your baby's development in each area. We know from experience that any loud, surprising sounds and sights can be upsetting for anyone. Realize that everything new is a surprise for a baby. For some, it can pique their interest and for others it can be disturbing. There are so many colourful and noise-filled infant toys out there, far more than when we grew up. We still somehow managed to grow and develop without them. Some of the simplest tried-and-true toys like colourful blocks and stacking toys, all-in-one play-stations with movable parts, swings with objects to bat at and move that fit over baby lying down still fit the bill. Computerized, battery-operated gizmos seem to me to be over-the-top and unnecessary. Being able to physically interact with, reach out and grab, easily make noise and have fun are prerequisites that any baby can enjoy.

To me, the most important ingredient in stimulating your baby's growth is your time with them. Providing every toy imaginable for them doesn't make up for you playing with them. Again, don't get me wrong…babies and children need to learn to be able to have fun on their own and enjoy their own company. Talking to them, naming things and helping them to direct their explorations, cheering on their efforts helps give them more of the tools and confidence to explore on their own. Playing pat-a-cake (does anyone even do that one anymore?), singing songs about body parts, giggling and laughing together while learning is a joy. Pots and pans are a wonderful (and free) thrill for little ones to bang. I can well remember the first time my son crawled over to the kitchen and pulled out the pots and pans, merrily banging on them with a huge grin on his face.

Of course, we know that every home has to be "baby-proofed" with a little one who is reaching out and touching their new world. Anything dangerous, toxic or hazardous absolutely must be moved out of their reach, but everything else is fair game!

Everything can and does go in their mouth once they can grab a hold of it. Little fingers can get into the most unexpected of places (like your eyes, your nose, your ears, your mouth!), as they explore everything.

Music can be a joy to share with your baby. Most love to be danced with or rocked to it. Again, watch the volume around those little developing ears!!! It can set a calming, relaxing tone for sleep- or nap-time. It can be a wonderful addition to play-time and sometimes be a great distraction if they're cranky.

Reading with your baby is a great opportunity to snuggle and get close. Using funny or different voices and making the sounds from the stories catches their interest and helps them remember. It can encourage a life-long interest in reading and learning and can become a great pastime for them on their own. We all have our favourites from our childhoods and many of these time-honoured classics are still out there. Parent-child reading times at libraries where staff or authors read their stories aloud and promote interaction are often great outings to do together all through childhood.

A word about baby-talk…it may sound cute to other adults, but don't do it. Babies and children repeat what they hear. Do you really want your baby to continue using it or do you want others to be able to understand them? Use the right words, not shortened or cute forms. If you use some sort of code-word for something with your child, who else is going to know to use it in order to communicate with them? Some examples are names for the bathroom and body parts…if they use those terms around others, people may not know what they're talking about or possibly ridicule them later on if they continue to use them. Watch the swear-words, too, as anything said loudly or forcefully is more likely to catch their attention and be repeated. All of us have heard potty-mouth from youngsters that is embarrassing for the parents and not at all cute or appropriate.

Remember those great puzzles we had as babies, with the chunky pieces that had little knobs on them to pull out and peek at what's underneath? Those are great toys to promote eye-hand coordination, stimulate memory and visual associations, teaching shapes and sizes and encouraging exploration. The same goes for blocks and stacking toys…things they can move and manipulate on their own. Another word of caution here: everything (and I mean everything!) is fair game for infants and young children to put into their mouths. If it's small enough to fit, they'll try it! Too-small objects are choking hazards for little ones. Yes, although it's a no-brainer, infants and small children still show up in emergency rooms having swallowed something they weren't supposed to, sometimes something toxic. Small objects will go into mouths, ears and noses if they can fit, so be vigilant. These things are preventable with common-sense and advance preparation.

Some parents begin parent-baby swim-times and classes are almost always available at community pools. Having a teacher/coach there to help and provide encouragement gives greater confidence for parents to try it out with their babies. I can remember my baby daughter's excitement (and my own as well!) as we took to the water together for the first time. Hugging her and seeing the thrill on her little face as she touched the water and let it move through her fingers, kicking her little legs in pleasure is a memory etched forever in my mind. You don't have to be a good swimmer as the classes are always held in the shallow end where you can stand comfortably. Giving your baby this experience in the water at a young age is a timeless gift as it becomes something they naturally develop a comfort for.

It's very important to not push any baby or child too far too fast. What I mean here is that muscle tone and strength develops as a baby is ready. If, for example, you try to get them to hold their head up too early, you can risk injury to their neck. The same goes for everything as they progress. Understand that babies' bones are malleable yet, meaning that they are still forming. The fontanelles at the top of their head (the soft spots in their skull which aren't fully closed yet until around age 2) were there to allow their heads to be squeezed through the birth canal. That means that you still have to be careful to protect them from head injury.

If a baby can't yet sit up on its own, don't push them. Prop them up and stay with them to catch them if they slide, to prevent any injury to their back, spine and head. If they can't roll over on their own yet, be extremely careful about leaving anything in their crib or playpen that they can't move away from if it comes too close to their face and mouth. You never know when they're going to achieve a milestone, and leaving a baby on a mat without supervision can have them roll over unexpectedly or begin creeping towards what you haven't yet baby-proofed.

Be prepared for the unexpected! Anything close to an edge can be pulled down or fall onto them. A baby being close to an edge can move and fall unexpectedly, causing any number of possible injuries. There is no safe place for an infant in that one moment of reaching for a diaper or a change of clothes. Every moment of a child in a bath-tub, whether a baby-tub or in a bath-seat needs supervision. A baby (child or adult) can drown in an inch of water in a matter of seconds. Anything they can reach can and will end up in their mouths, that's a given

Above all, love every moment of this first year together of amazing growth for all of you. Be your baby's best cheerleader and enthusiastically let them know how amazing they are!!! Every attempt, every movement and sound they make is a step closer to every great moment ahead! All of this up to that First Birthday cake, jammed into their little mouths (ears, noses, eyes, hair!) with joy and pride...now that's a picture you'll always remember!

Chapter 10
Toddlerhood: Who says there are Terrible Twos?

You now have a toddler on your hands, with the independence of greater mobility and their own mind, to-boot! Keeping up with a little one who has a greater length of "umbilical cord" or comfortable distance from you can be a challenge. They can and will get into so much more. It's their way of exploring and learning about everything around them. Encouraging them while keeping them safe is the great balancing act, as you want them to grow through experiences, but they still don't understand the potential dangers in their environment.

With their greater use and comprehension of language, we can begin to understand better what is going on in a child's mind. Opening up that window, being able to understand what they're trying to say, not just by their actions is an amazing leap forward to knowing your child. Expressing themselves with single words is a huge first step, but then piecing them together into 2- and 3-word sentences takes things to a new level. Now, you can start to piece together their thought-processes and it becomes even more exciting!

Babies and then toddlers will chat to themselves as a running patter and it's fascinating to hear them. As we've all heard, twin babies will sometimes even develop their own language that only they can understand. Learning your own child's language, what they're telling themselves and trying to tell you can be like deciphering a code but once you've got it figured out, it's all uphill from there! Parents learn to help their child to express themselves and to be understood, but sometimes it's not as easy for others. I have seen and experienced many times when parents have "translated" or explained what their child is saying to others, to decrease the frustration with not being understood. Just like we encourage others to be patient in listening and repeating back what they think they've heard, we need to be patient with our child and ourselves throughout this process.

Hearing you little one say "no" for the first time is adorable, assuming they know what it means. It also starts to show off their growing decision-making ability and preferences. Working through a toddler's refusal to eat or do something like dressing or clearing up their toys can be a challenge. Just because they seem to understand so much more, don't assume they understand your explanation for why it needs to be done or happen. Talking beyond their level of comprehension only serves to fuel the frustration for you both.

Making it fun to dress or clean up sometimes alleviates a tense situation. Distraction to another task can also often achieve your goal. For instance, if you want the toy-room to be cleaned up but you get a "no!", go on to doing something else and then return to the task. You may then have them in a mood to comply. Accomplishing things together like a team will often encourage them to try something, like taking a bite of the food they're refusing to eat, yourself. If they see you "like it", they are more likely to try it, too.

Use your Imagination!

With your child's greater language skills and ability to express themselves, they can let us into their imaginary world. It is a wonderful world where all possibilities exist to be anything and do anything with no boundaries. Stimulating and entering into your child's imaginary world is an amazing experience. There, they can try out any activity, any identity, any skill, any place, any career or adventure. Nothing stands in their way and they can do what may seem to be the impossible. Let them and join in the fun!

Children learn by play and experience and it doesn't have to be real to us. Dressing or styling themselves as pirates, princesses, astronauts, ballet dancers, cowboys or cowgirls, chefs, models or mad scientists among many others allows them to try out different identities, new imaginary places and skills. Engage with them and join their world if they'll let you. It may seem like silliness to pretend along as a fellow traveller on an imaginary journey or adventure, but it's not at all.

Fantasy is linked to reality. If a person could not imagine flying to the moon, would we have ever have gotten there? If a famous sports figure hadn't imagined themselves being a star, would they have gotten there? The power of positive thinking, imagining the "what ifs" becoming possible is what has fuelled human endeavour since the beginning of time.

Creativity has to begin with imagination. It takes us out-of-bounds of what we know, to be able to envision something different. Enriching your child's creativity by joining in and providing props or tools like costumes or even boxes to be used as furniture or objects fuels their imaginations even further. They feel empowered, confident and important as they play the part. Many parents follow up on these themes in children's bedrooms with pirate rooms, princess rooms, race-car rooms, space rooms with stars on the ceiling and mobiles of the solar system, rooms with an under-the-sea theme for aspiring young marine biologists. Embracing and playing along shows your child that you value their creativity and imagination.

Practice makes perfect, doesn't it? Athletes, musicians and other performing artists use their imagination to see themselves making the perfect shot, singing the perfect note or playing the perfect part. Business people rehearse the perfect presentation in their minds, even suitors practice the perfect proposal in advance hoping for and imagining a "yes". It is a way of rehearsing internally and preparing for the real thing, seeing and feeling the success as many times as you want to propel you to success.

Temper Tantrums

Now let's turn to the biggest example of what people call the "Terrible Twos"...temper tantrums. We've all seen them happening in grocery stores or wherever parents are trying to encourage their children to leave someplace they're having fun. Everyone has a solution to how to deal with them, their own spin on how to shorten or eliminate them. It is not simply the action of a child who is spoiled and wants their own way.

It's very important to explain and understand the underlying reason behind a "tantrum" or melt-down. We know that this is a big spreading-their wings, independence phase for a child. They are learning that not only can things be done for them by others when they communicate what they want, but they are beginning to be able to do things for themselves. They are no longer as helpless or dependent. They still want what they want and have the vocabulary to express it sometimes (or by their behaviours!).

What if they still have a hard time expressing is their emotions? Our emotional vocabulary is so personal, so complex, sometimes even as adults too hard to put into words. Imagine a little one trying to sort out for themselves all of what they are feeling and then trying to it into words! That in itself can be incredibly frustrating! How many times have we all struggled with expressing ourselves when our emotions are so intense? The wrong words come out or no words at all as we shake in frustration...

Put all of that into the little body of someone who is just starting to be able to express themselves. The more confused and frustrated they become, the worse it gets. Have you ever experienced or witnessed someone who is crying in anger or frustration? The immediate reaction to someone crying is to reach out and try to comfort them, but look out, because that's not what they want!!! Those tears of anger or frustration are not a signal to approach, they're a signal to give them some space to collect themselves. This is no different.

So what to do? You have a tantrum on your hands. You're frustrated and so obviously is your little one. In the short-term, depending upon where you are, either give them some space to calm down or leave the situation with them. I think we've all seen more than our share of moms (or dads) leaving a grocery store, their full cart left behind with a tantrumming toddler in tow. Removing them (and yourself) from the stares of others and perhaps unwanted suggestions or advice allows cooler heads to prevail. You are the adult and your child is looking to you to help them calm down. Losing it, yourself only escalates the situation and certainly doesn't provide the best role-model. Don't drive off in frustration, wait a bit to calm your nerves and know that this too, shall pass.

If it happens at home and you have the time, wait it out, making sure that your little one can't hurt themselves throwing themselves around on the floor. Once it's out of their system, they'll be able to think more clearly and express themselves better. When things are calmer, approach them or wait for them to come to you and talk quietly with them about what they're trying to express. Help them to be able to communicate without acting out.

Giving your youngster a "feelings vocabulary" is so important in the early years. The more they can express their own and recognize other's feelings, the better their ability to relate to others. Some of the greatest miscommunication between adults comes from misunderstanding or making assumptions about how someone else is feeling. We operate or respond based on what we think they're feeling, but if we're wrong, our responses will be wrong. Being able to "read" others is one of the greatest tools to helping people understand each other.

All of us have seen "feelings posters" on the internet that show facial expressions on a character with the emotions written below. This is a fantastic game to play with your child, asking what the faces show. Extending this to showing emotional reactions on your face and having them guess what it means is a lot of fun and a terrific teaching tool. Similarly, having them play the game by showing facial expressions and asking you recognize them teaches them how others "read" them and helps them to learn new words to express how they're feeling. The more they can express, the less frustrated they'll feel at not being understood. "Use your words" becomes a familiar refrain to encourage this new skill.

Probably the best advice about a tantrum in the short-term is don't let it escalate. Try and remember that it's probably frustration and increasing it only makes it worse for you both. "Giving in" to a tantrum in the short-term (letting them have what they may want) only teaches them that it works. If it has worked for them, children will continue to do it and it may last longer as they struggle to get you to give in. Once you've given in (and they hope you will!), all that does is strengthen the behaviour because it works. The duration can become longer and longer, with the expectation that you'll eventually give in. If they "win" from a long one, they'll keep getting longer, anticipating that you'll continue to give up in order to appease them. Don't let it happen. Stick to the plan and approach when they're calmer and you're able to reason with them.

There is nothing wrong with giving children choices about certain things. Who cares if they want to wear blue instead of red today? It helps give them a sense that their preferences are being heard and acknowledged. Do they want their meal in the yellow bowl or the orange one? Does it really matter, as long as they're eating? There are many things that they do not have a choice about doing, however…having a bath or bed-time, for example. These can become a battle-ground as they are more able to express themselves. Setting a line at what you decide and what they can help decide is important.

Being involved in making choices builds confidence but giving too much say on matters such as when to go to bed, when to eat, whether to take a bath or not can actually creates a false sense of control when it comes to your child entering into the outside world. There will be rules and expectations out there, whether in school or playing at other children's homes. Your child does not have a choice there to listen or agree or not. What teacher has the time to cajole each child in the classroom to complete an assignment or not? What parent wants to battle with someone else's child who is over to play at their home and refuses to take off their shoes when they come inside or demands a snack when they want it and won't take "no" for an answer? Who can afford to say "no" to a boss when they've been told to complete a job?

Toilet-Training:

Although toilet-training requires advanced muscle development, the social and emotional importance of it requires special attention. No one likes diapers, least of all children. Finally being free of wearing a diaper is a huge boost to a child's self-esteem (as well as one less chore for parents!). It makes outings more flexible (although you always have to know where the nearest washroom is and check that they've "gone" before you leave!), and is seen as a big developmental step.

Every child has their own progression of development unlike any other. Just because your friend's child or a family member's child is toilet-trained doesn't mean there's anything wrong with yours if they've not yet. It is a natural part of life and requires, like any new development, muscle control and sensation. It begins with figuring out your child's natural schedule after and between eating. Introducing the potty for the first time creates excitement and anticipation for parents and children and always needs to be a positive place. There can never be any shame about "missing" or forgetting. Every attempt needs to be encouraged and celebrated.

Placing your child on the potty and reading together or chatting or singing, whatever makes it a positive experience, encourages them to want to "go" there. Even peeing beside them on the toilet at the same time models for them how "big people" go. In the beginning, you are the one who tries to figure out when they might have to go, to encourage success of a pee or a poo on the potty. Over time, your child will begin to recognize for themselves when they have to go and reward you with a self-motivated trip to the potty. Talking with them about how it feels inside when they have to go helps them make the connection for themselves.

From day-time dryness (rewarded with "big-girl/big-boy" underwear) to dry nights is a big step. Remember, they are just learning to be aware of their bodies when they're awake. Doing it at night-time when they're asleep really needs your help for success, by ensuring a good turn on the potty before bed and less liquids by a certain time before bed. Every dry night is to be celebrated, just like dry days, because it's even harder!

Having a potty close-by is easier for a child than a child seat on the toilet. The time it takes for them to take down their pants and hop up on the toilet depends upon how badly they have to go and their size to get up there. Remember that. Set them up for success.

What if your child isn't catching on very fast? It can be frustrating for you and for them. Achieving this milestone is a big one for their self-esteem, for school and for their social life. A child who is still in diapers while their age-mates are using the toilet is bound to feel some embarrassment. Toileting should **never** involve shame. It is a natural process that they will learn. If you have any concerns, consult your doctor, as some children have weaker bladders that still need to develop to make it easier for them to "hold it".

Make them want to succeed by making toileting a positive experience. Share in their successes by telling the other parent so they can cheer them on, as well. **Just like in every aspect of your child's development, cheer on every attempt to try…don't point out the failures or "misses".** You will get there together. As huge an issue as this may seem to be now, it will be forgotten in the long-run. There are so many other areas of development that are happening for you to cheer about!

Developmental Concerns

An infant and then a toddler and child's health needs to be monitored by your doctor at every step of the way. If you have concerns, always be ready to talk about them. Their vision and hearing need to be checked regularly. I can't stress this enough. Just because a little one can't read yet doesn't mean that their **vision** can't be checked. A child who can't see clearly is at a huge disadvantage in their world. They don't know that what they're seeing (or not seeing) isn't "normal" and wouldn't know what to say if their vision isn't clear. They have nothing to compare it to. If you suspect some difficulty, get your physician to examine them and make a referral to a vision care professional.

Your child's **hearing** is as important as their vision. Ask any parent of a toddler who just doesn't seem to "listen" if they've asked their doctor to check on it. Many times, they just choose not to listen, but sometimes hearing issues can get in the way. If your little one has experienced a lot of ear infections or has tubes in their ear canals to help with them, they may have experienced times when their hearing didn't work for them reliably and they may have come to not rely on this sense. Your doctor may make a referral to an audiologist to pinpoint what, if any areas are of concern. They can then, in turn, help you to understand and work with or around any hearing issues.

Hearing a watery or muffled world through infections can be confusing and irritating and they can sometimes choose to "turn it off" or not listen. A child who has not had consistent information from their hearing may be more likely to focus on their vision to process information around them. These children may become "visual learners" over time, not expecting consistent information from their hearing.

Patient reminders to refocus your child on using their ears, with visual cues to listen can help them to learn to use and trust their hearing again. Understand that it doesn't take a profound hearing loss to cause a child to ignore or minimize what they hear. If you're not sure, again, check with the professionals to ensure everything is working fine.

Speech issues can sometimes be closely related to hearing. We need to be able to hear what others are saying clearly to respond to them and to mimic what we hear. If you notice that your child's speech is slow to develop, hard to hear or to understand, have them seen by a professional. It may be linked to hearing issues or other developmental concerns. A referral to a speech and language pathologist can give you some great help to encourage speech and language development. Working together on in-patient appointments and home-work assignments they create for you will help immensely to encourage growth in your child's ability to communicate.

Any concerns with **physical** development should be discussed with your doctor. There may be family patterns of development that you see coming out in your child that are of concern to you. Strength, coordination and muscle tone can all impact on attaining developmental milestones. If your doctor has concerns with your child relative to "normal" development, they may do further testing and/or suggest a referral to other professionals like physiotherapists and occupational therapists who can help target the areas needing some strengthening in development. Like speech and language pathologists, they will help you develop and practice programs at home to work on areas requiring added help.

Self-Confidence

Building your toddler's self-confidence is a gift that we give them to carry into their future. If they don't believe in themselves, if we don't believe in them, who is going to? Lots of encouragement when you see them trying, teaching them to encourage and cheer themselves on helps create the drive to continue. At this young age, they'll make lots of mistakes but that's okay, because they're just learning. If they miss the potty when peeing, miss their mouths when feeding themselves, get their shoes on the wrong feet, encourage them by telling them it's great that they're trying and keep at it! Just like any good coach, pointing out the effort, not the failures will create a supportive and positive environment to keep trying and improving. Teach them to be their own cheer-leaders, too.

With greater mobility and comprehension, it's now time to help your little one to become a part of the family "team". It goes a long way towards empowering them to feel a member of the family and helpful at the same time. It also sets the stage for doing "chores" as they grow older, learning to take care of themselves and help out others at the same time. Obviously, what I'm talking about here is age-appropriate tasks that they can do, like helping to pick up their toys. Making it as easy as possible with baskets and bins, cupboards or closets, work together to make it a game and let them know how much you appreciate it. Let them "help" put the laundry in the washer, "help" pick up leaves as you rake the garden, put their dishes by the sink (if they can reach) after a meal.

It will probably take longer with their help, but the pride that they feel at being able to take part propels little ones to want to do more. They don't understand yet that the more they learn to do for themselves, the better it is for them in the future or that the less you will have to do on your own, the more time you have to spend with them. That will come with time. All they know is that it makes you happy and they feel good about themselves and then doesn't everyone win?

The joys of seeing your baby become a toddler far outweigh the frustrations. They are becoming their own person, able to interact with you and their own world more, able to understand and be understood. Remember that it is a complex and confusing world that they're entering, filled with rules and expectations that they're trying to understand. You are their teachers, interpreters and cruise directors on their journey into the world. At the same time, you're learning to understand the complex little person who you helped create. Genetics and environment combine to make us who we are. We can't change the genetics, but how nurturing, understanding, patient and positive we are with a youngster goes a long way to helping them to become the happiest and most confident they can be.

Chapter 11

The Pre-School Years: Preparing in every way

The next big leap ahead for a toddler is helping to prepare them for school. We have examined strategies to encourage emotional, intellectual and social development up to this point. We'll look to further strengthen these areas with an eye towards preparing them for the school years ahead. After all, the more prepared they can be for the expectations of the educational system, the better.

Emotional Development:

The focus on emotional development has been on helping your little one to be able to understand and express their emotions as well as those of others. As they get older, they will interact with more and more people both in and outside the home. Spreading their wings, they will try new things and new experiences. Having that emotional vocabulary to express how they feel, what they want and what they need gives them even greater self-confidence and assertiveness.

Let's talk about assertiveness, how it relates to children. Being assertive means being able to say what you feel, what you want and what you need. It is not aggressiveness, which means trying to get what you want at the expense of others. No one wants their child to be aggressive. Nor do we want to see a passive child, quietly not expressing themselves about how they feel. That can lead to a lifetime of misunderstanding and frustration, as they see others get what they want and they can't begin to know how to ask. Passivity can also lead to aggressiveness out of the frustration of holding back emotions until they burst out.

Teaching children to express themselves if they don't already do so involves patience, gentle questioning and empowering them to speak up for themselves. They may not get what they want, but being able to say how they feel about it and why is a very important developmental step. At the same time, teaching them that others have feelings that may be different in a situation helps them gain a better sense of themselves and others.

As an example, if a child wants to go out and play but the weather is too cold, being told "no" can trigger a reaction. But they want to and they got to go outside yesterday! Explaining that it is too cold out and you worry about them catching a cold may not satisfy them, but it does show them that others have feelings and opinions, as well. Remind them that everyone has feelings, and maybe even ask them how they would feel if they were you. Sometimes, role-playing situations in reverse, with you playing their role and them as the parent can help them to understand. It can also be a lovely distraction at the same time, encouraging play with you inside.

Being able to express themselves and empathize with others is the beginning to a successful social life, as well. We all know that toddlers and pre-schoolers are notorious about having problems with sharing. Being around other people does require all of us to be able to share and is a big step towards getting along with others. They will have to be able to get along with others in school, on the playground, in the family, with play-mates, and in other activities. It doesn't come naturally for everyone so the more you can practice with them, the faster they'll learn.

You can encourage sharing by modelling it, yourself and talking it through. For example, let's say that your little one wants a bite of something you're eating. You can say that it's yours and you don't want to share, explaining that you understand how they feel (they want some!). You can say that it's yours, but you'd be happy to share because it will make them happy. Both show that you have feelings and that you recognize theirs, as well. Similarly, joining in something that they're playing, you ask if you can share with them. If they welcome you to playing with them, cheer them on for their willingness to share and let them know how good this makes them feel. They'll feel good about it, too! If they refuse, let them know how it hurts your feelings, that playing together is fun for both of you. They will see that it is a win-win situation.

Over time, they will come to understand that others have feelings too and take them into consideration. However, youngsters are naturally egocentric (self-focused), so unless prompted, they may not have even thought about how others feel. By you reminding them ("How do you think Mummy/Daddy/friend feels?"), they will eventually naturally start to think about it, as well.

Social Development:

Closely monitoring play-time with other children and catching these potential "sharing" moments is extremely important. Praise them for their kindness and remind them that it makes it more fun for everyone. The development from "parallel play" (children playing beside each other but not interacting) to interactive play is a huge step along the road to a healthy social life.

We can clearly see that encouraging play-dates, attending play-groups and group activities like pre-school gym classes or swim classes (among many other options) gives children the opportunity to grow and develop their social skills. While we want them to be open to meeting new children, sharing and being assertive, we also want them to keep themselves safe.

An open, engaging child welcomes attention and interacts with everyone. They are not fearful of strangers and while this is probably fine when you're around them, it leaves them open to possible dangers in the world out there. It is no secret that we live in a more dangerous world than when we grew up. There are predators out there who can hurt or take away our children. We have seen more than our share of Amber Alerts, of kidnappings, children who are lost and never found. This is the reality of our world and we can't think that it can never happen to us. Preparing your child to protect themselves from unwanted advances is a critical skill for their survival. If they never need to use these skills, that's wonderful but if they do, isn't it better that they know what to do?

Teaching children that strangers can be nice or dangerous is a first step. There are some great programs out in the schools right now where children learn that someone who looks "nice" may not be and someone who doesn't look "nice" may actually be nice. It never hurts to be prepared, and child-proofing your little one before school begins is important. Predators know that younger children are more vulnerable. While we don't want a child to be paranoid, terrified of any strangers, we want to teach them to be cautious and not assume they are kind. Not approaching strangers is a great rule. Ignoring their advances if they persist is another great one, teaching them to run to a safe place (Block Parents, homes that have that sign on them is important for them to learn about) is another really good one. If someone does try to grab them, teaching your child to yell, bite, kick and run is critical for them to save themselves. Knowing these skills and role-playing them with your child strengthens their ability to react in a situation. The more a skill is practiced and learned, the easier it is to use it, even if in a panic.

Going to play-dates at other homes exposes children to other families' rules. If you haven't had the children playing together already at your home, talking with the other parent first to reinforce what's okay in your home can help ease any confusion. You may not allow them to play unsupervised on a different floor yet while the other home is different. You may not allow snacks at certain times or certain foods. Sending along an appropriate snack from your home may help avoid this in advance. You may be in the middle of toilet-training and have a regular schedule for "going on the potty" during the day. The other child may be toilet-training, as well or not or may be toilet-trained already. Discuss this in advance to avoid confusion. Every play experience outside of the home gives your child new opportunities to practice their social skills and to learn to get along with others.

Physical Development:

Your child is gaining greater strength and muscle development as they get older. Working on small-muscle development and fine-motor skills will help them prepare for the tasks of gluing, cutting with scissors, colouring, printing and writing when they reach school. Doing creative activities with children at home that involve these skills is a lot of fun and helps them to get better with time and practice. Little ones are very proud when they're doing "school" at home!

Creativity is the key and it doesn't take a lot of expensive tools to begin. Gluing macaroni on paper (without them eating the glue!) is a great beginner task. Colouring in colouring books together or on blank pieces of paper can be a lot of fun. Cutting with safety scissors around shapes you draw on paper takes a lot of coordination. Gluing these on paper afterwards works on both skills. Tracing letters that you've taught them to name from reading together is a great beginning. It can begin with your holding their little hands as you trace together and then eventually with them doing it on their own. Teaching your child to recognize and learn to write their name is a huge accomplishment that they will proudly practice over and over.

Proudly displaying their efforts on the fridge helps children feel good about their efforts, promoting healthy self-esteem. Being a "big kid" and doing their "homework" together helps your child feel like they're getting ready for the excitement of school ahead.

Large muscle development involves coordination, too. Being able to catch and throw a ball, jump, skip and kick a ball are all skills that promote this development and will be used in sports and activities in the future. Just like fine-motor, small-muscle skills, there are fun ways to promote development of each skill. Your child can already grab and hold a ball, how about rolling one toward each other between your legs, so that they can time their "catch" with the ball's movement and speed? Having mastered that skill, standing and throwing and catching is the next logical step. Larger, softer balls made of sponge or soft plastic don't hurt so much if they're missed and hit someone or something.

They've probably already mastered running and love being chased around the house, yard or park. Jumping games, like on a safe, supervised trampoline, help with balance and coordination. Skipping requires even more coordination, as it makes them have to think about each step, jumping and bouncing from one side to the other. Skipping with a jump-rope is even more complicated as they have to figure out the timing of their jumps while twirling the rope around themselves. Think about it…it's not easy! Just like the timing of catching a ball and skipping, kicking a ball is no small feat. Knowing when the ball is going to hit their foot, how to stop it, and how to kick it where takes a lot of coordination.

You can see how each of these skills can be learned in a fun way. Each of them translates into many sports and other activities. The more your child is prepared and has developed coordination, the more fun they will have playing with other children and in organized activities and sports. Don't assume they will naturally be good at these skills…some may be, but not everyone. Give your child the advantage of mastery and self-confidence by playing games together that encourage these skills.

Now, a little bit about sportsmanship…not everyone is good at every sport or even at any one sport. Teach your child that it's okay to try their best and they should be proud of themselves. At the same time, teach them to be kind when it comes to others when they play games or sports. Like I said, not everyone is athletic, but everyone deserves to have a good time playing. I think all of us can remember the kids (it may even have been us) who were picked last for teams. It's pretty devastating and not something easily forgotten.

Intellectual Development:

We've already talked about working on the fine-motor and social skills that promote your child's successful transition into school. What about the academic expectations? Preparing your child for the intellectual curiosity and desire to learn has already begun from the day they were born. They naturally want to learn and do so with every touch, every look, every listen. They are primed to learn by every experience as they gain knowledge about their world around them.

Talking to your child about their experiences, what is going on in the world around them helps open up their world even more. It encourages them to share their thoughts and ideas, to ask questions, and to want to learn more. Of course, television is a ready source of information that may not require much other than passively watching, but teaching your child a love of reading with age-appropriate books from an early age motivates them to want to decipher what letters and words mean. The same goes for computers, with the huge market of computer-learning games available.

Certainly, in today's world, key-boarding skills on the computer are invaluable for the explosion of information available there, but I still can see no substitute for physically holding a book, turning the pages and reciting or reading along. Growing up around books, seeing family read them, magazines or the newspaper encourages little ones to want to do the same. Every effort to "read" along as you read to them needs to be recognized and celebrated. Some of it may be simple memorization of the order of the story or the words, but it is the beginning of wanting to understand what it says.

There are two strategies to reading words: whole-word recognition and decoding. Word recognition happens from memorizing what they look like as you read along out-loud. It is a starting point that is so exciting when your child "knows" what a word looks like! The more books you read together, the more words they are exposed to and the greater chance to recognize words.

Decoding or "sounding out" words requires more understanding of the sounds each letter makes, the multitude of rules surrounding it. It must of course begin with recognizing letters (the ABCs) and the sounds they make alone and together. There are many fun books, games and activities for learning the association of letters with the sounds they make and you can play them while going on outings, on drives, while preparing meals, just about anywhere. Realize that it takes a lot of intellectual sophistication to understand that these symbols ("letters") represent sounds that put together make words. Do not take this intellectual leap-of-faith for granted!

Of course, going to the library and sharing in story-times there helps encourage a love for stories and books. Having a library card for the first time can be a very proud moment for any little one. The smorgasbord of books available at a library abounds and is much more than any parent could afford to buy, but there will always be special ones that become favourites for bedtime that you just have to buy.

The search for knowledge becomes exponential as a child grows. Encouraging this thirst with books and trips to museums, zoos, to parks and out into nature stimulates even more questions. Encourage questions and if you don't know the answer, look it up together in books or on the internet. A lifetime of seeking answers and knowledge is never lost, as we learn well up until our last day on earth.

Remember that a child's attention span gets longer as they grow. It may seem that they flit from one thing to another when they're little, but they will be able to focus for longer periods of time as they grow. Of course, learning requires being able to pay attention and focus. If your child doesn't seem to pay attention to tasks for long, encourage them to stay at it. Realize that school requires them to focus for varying periods of time on subjects that may or may not interest them. This is an acquired skill that you can help them learn with practice.

Organizational or planning skills are also extremely important in school and at almost any task. Teaching your child to approach doing something with a plan in mind is a life-long skill. After all, who can accomplish more complex things like making a meal or doing their taxes without some plan of attack? Teaching a youngster to approach a task in an organized manner can be accomplished with having them first verbalize out loud what they need (tools, items) to complete it. Once having collected what they need, they talk or coach themselves through each of the steps to completing the task. This self-talk is something we have learned to do inside our own minds with everything we do. We may not realize it anymore as it is automatic, but it's how we worked through doing things for the first time.

Let's take an example. Your child may want to colour a picture in a colouring book. Help them talk out loud to themselves what they need to do this. They need the book, their crayons and a table and chair. Talk them through (by example) getting everything together. Think-out-loud the steps they may take once they have everything to approach the picture. They may want to approach it by color or the outline first. Have them talk through their thoughts as they progress until they're done. Once they're finished, don't forget to talk them through putting everything away!

This strategy can be extended to more complicated tasks like cooking or baking a recipe, doing laundry or building something. Making a recipe requires having all of the necessary ingredients available and the measuring tools to put in the right amounts, as well as the tools, bowls and pots or pans to cook them in. We do it without even thinking as we read through a recipe, but having your "little helper" nearby working through each step teaches them the organization of things and steps to work towards making something. The pride and joy at cooking together, the finished product proudly displayed and eaten by the family, something that they've been involved in making contributes greatly to a child's self-esteem.

More about cooking, baking and building...learning to measure and what numbers and fractions mean in everyday life is a great beginning to early arithmetic/math. Who didn't learn fractions for the first time with a teacher using "pieces of a pie" as an example? Using a ruler can begin with using a measuring tape or ruler at home as they help "fix" things around the house. It gives numbers meaning, not just as abstract concepts.

Boys & Girls

I am a firm believer that although there are some fundamental anatomical differences between boys and girls, we are much more alike than different. There is more variability between individual boys and girls than there is between the two sexes. Having toys available that are "gender neutral" so that not only little girls play with dolls and little boys play with cars and trucks is not a new phenomenon but some parents still worry that their girl may become a "tomboy" or their boy will become a "sissy". To say that the lines are now blurred between men and women in terms of jobs and careers is an understatement. Giving your child the message that they can be anything they want to be is an important one.

Don't worry if your little boy wants to play dress-up. Don't worry if your little girl loves to play with cars or trucks. They are exploring their world and what they enjoy. There are role-models out there who excel in all areas in both genders. Let them figure out for themselves what they enjoy doing, what they're good at. Popular "wisdom" out there used to limit girls to being under-achievers in math or sports. Boys weren't encouraged to cook or sew. It was seen as too "feminine". Now look at what no boundaries have allowed us to do! The pioneers in varying professions have led the way for anyone to succeed, "unhampered" by gender. What parent wouldn't be proud of a son who is famous chef or designer? What parent wouldn't be proud of a daughter who is an engineer or an astronaut?

I am also a firm believer in boys and girls playing together, which helps in those early years of school, in the first attempts at dating and in the friendship of a marriage. We are all ignorant of what we don't know about and we learn by experience. Encouraging your child to play with both boys and girls breaks down the barriers of what they don't know or haven't experienced. Sharing in the games that each play creates more variety of fun and friendships. It teaches them skills that each may learn from the other...physical sports helping them develop coordination and large muscle strength, creative activities fine-tuning fine-motor control and creativity. Who can't benefit from a combination of the two?

Encouraging your child to play with children of both genders takes the mystery out of the opposite sex. It teaches girls that boys can be gentle and boys that girls can be strong. It breaks down barriers and stereotypes. For boys who don't already have a sister they're comfortable playing with or girls who similarly don't have a brother, or kids who don't have cousins to play with, they can learn to play and have fun with each other. Isn't today's world filled with images of strong women and sensitive men? It broadens the availability of friends with similar interests when boys and girls play with each other and then no one needs to be left alone on the school playground. Encouraging your child to play with children of both genders helps them grow socially and to understand all children better.

Bullying

Bullying is an ugly reality in schoolyards and in any possible social situation for both children and adults. It happens in the workplace, at all school levels, and almost every place where people interact. Preparing your child in advance, when they begin to play with others and before entering school helps them to recognize it and react in ways that help protect them. Bully-proofing your child also helps prevent them from bullying behaviours, acknowledging their feelings and teaching them better ways to express their feelings. Let's also not forget about teaching children to back each other up. Sometimes all it takes for a child to stand up to or avoid bullying is for a bystander to say something. Children who have experienced bullying feel so isolated, as others look away or don't want to get involved. If someone, anyone has the compassion and kindness to say something, it can make a huge difference.

We've already talked about nurturing your child's emotional self and feelings vocabulary. Teaching them to use their words and not their hands or fists to express upset and frustration at not getting what they want or their way is a big step in the right direction. Teaching them empathy or an ability to understand that other people have feelings shows them how to take others into account. Bullies are frustrated and feel misunderstood. They don't understand how to get what they want or that other people have a right to their own feelings, wants, and needs, as well. Assertiveness training, teaching a child to express how they feel, what they want and what they need without being aggressive or passively enduring or waiting for something to happen gives them a big advantage in the world.

Role-modelling, rehearsing or "pretending" situations where a child may be picked on or bullied and presenting ways to deal with it gives them confidence. Present different scenarios with them with you being pushy on a playground to get on the slide or taking a toy your child wants to play with. Suggest different ways of dealing with it and have them try them out. Have them try to take a toy or a turn away from you and act out how a child can react to successfully rebuff a bully or being pushed around. The more it comes naturally for them in imaginary practice, the readier they will be to successfully address a situation.

Help your child understand that while being bullied feels like a personal attack, it is not about them but about what the other child wants. Knowing that it is not their issue, that they are not necessarily being targeted alone helps them feel less victimized. Encourage them to talk to you or another adult if strategies you have taught them don't work so that they don't suffer in silence. The cycle of bullying and being bullied must be caught early, before it creates children who feel like victims.

Chapter 12

School: The early years

Seeing your child go off to school for the first time is an emotional experience for you both. They are off in the world outside of the safety of your protected environment and learning the rules of school life socially and within the classroom. You've done your best to prepare yourself and them, but that first little while can be tough on you both. They're filled with excitement at being "big kids" now, but being away from what they know and understand can be difficult.

Some children have a harder time adjusting to being at school for the first time and there may be tears or fears at seeing you leave. Walking away from them, entrusting them to the teacher to take care of them can be especially difficult if they haven't been in a daycare, day-home, play-school or pre-school before. Preparing them (and yourself) for this next big step in their lives is important. Of course, a visit to the new school in advance already makes it a less scary place.

Going out together to buy those first school supplies, whether a backpack and lunch-kit, new school shoes and first-day outfit, is an exciting beginning. It makes your little one feel like a big kid, seeing the things they will use in their new place. Of course, lots of talking about the fun times and experiences ahead with new children to play with, new books and toys and new things to learn makes it seem all the more exciting.

To help them with the continuity from home of feeling apart from you, I suggest attaching a "transitional object" to their backpack or perhaps to their lunch-kit. It can be a teddy bear on a carabiner, a photo of the family together in a luggage tag attached to their backpack, a sticker on their lunch-kit that helps remind them that you're still there. Being away from you can feel detached for them and can be scary. Seeing this reminds them that just because you're not there <u>with</u> them, you are still there <u>for</u> them.

If your child's school is in your neighbourhood, hopefully there will be other children they know who are going to the same school. Play-dates and getting together with them in advance gives your child the safety net of already knowing someone there. You may even want to caravan together with the other family so that the children can be there together for the first time. Familiarity with people helps with any transition, giving some comfort from the beginning.

You may have had a chance to do an orientation at the school beforehand, visiting a classroom for your child to see where they're going to begin. Again, being familiar with people and surroundings in advance can help allay any fears or anxieties of a new place or situation. If you haven't had a chance to visit already, go for a walk around the school-yard so your child can see where they'll be playing at recesses and lining up to go inside. The more they recognize and are familiar with their surroundings, the more prepared they will be.

Getting to know your child's teacher is extremely important in every grade. He or she will be able to see your interest and concern in your child, that you want to work together as a team. It is a team effort in school, working closely with the teacher to help them understand your child and to learn from them what they see and need help with in the classroom. Understanding their expectations and rules allows you to follow up and reinforce them at home. That way, you can help work through any misunderstanding in rules or expectations. Just like we work together in a team as parents, your child needs to understand that you and their teacher are working together to help them learn.

The teacher will let you know how things are going socially, emotionally and academically with your child. If you don't know, ask. They are there to help. Some children talk excitedly about their days, letting you know what has happened. Encourage this, as it is your window on their new world. If they don't talk about it, ask them. If you get no response or a "fine", ask the teacher or other parents. My children were always very chatty and informative about their days at school and often, other parents would call to find out what was happening because their children weren't telling them. Try calling other parents for their "take" on things.

If you have concerns or your child seems upset or sad, set up a meeting with their teacher or chat with them after class. The more the teacher knows and the more you know, the better you can work together to make your child's school days happy and successful. The teacher can help work on any areas of concern at school and give you ideas to work on them at home.

If school-work seems hard for them, ask the teacher to get some ideas of how to practice skills at home. "Homework" doesn't have to be onerous, it can be seen as a fun time to do school-work together, for your child to share their new world with you. It's a "big kid" thing that you can work on with a drink and a snack after school or after dinner. You could also do your own "homework" or paperwork beside them at the kitchen table. It may even be going through mail and paying bills, but it shows them that they're not alone.

If your child is having trouble making friends or has social issues with another child at school, talk to their teacher about it. They may be surprised to hear it, as they may find your child is socializing just fine and playing comfortably with others. Sometimes when a child says they're feeling "lonely" or "have no friends", the truth is that they do but don't recognize it. Reminding them about what their teacher says can help them to feel better. If they truly don't seem to interact much or tend to keep to themselves, ask the teacher for some suggestions of how to help. He or she may try to pair them up with a buddy or group in the classroom to create more opportunities for developing friendships. Your teacher may also suggest a growing friendship they see with another child and you can help this along by suggesting to that child's parents about arranging a play-date. The more you can do to help, the better.

With attention to your child's school life, both academic and social, you can help them make this a great new, successful experience. Working together with the teacher and other parents, you can become a part of your child's positive school experience. If you have or can make the time, volunteering at their school for outings, parent classroom days, in the library, for sports days or anything you can lets you in on their world, to share their experiences. Children whose parents attend and volunteer at their schools are always so excited to introduce them to the other children and teachers and to introduce everyone to you. It is a wonderful way of making home part of school and school part of home.

All through the school years, make sure to attend parent-teacher meetings. If you can't make the times available, try to schedule something else with your child's teacher. These meetings allow you to understand how your child is developing and performing at school, far more than a report card alone. If your spouse can't make it, take notes so that you can tell them about it and they can stay on-track along with you and the teacher. If your child can attend these meetings with you, they can show you their classroom and accomplishments and hear what their teacher has to say. It helps reinforce for them the team effort between home and school.

Expectations & Performance:

Every classroom and every school is different. Teachers and schools have their own "personalities", different cultures and environments. What they do have in common is a recognized curriculum of expectations for learning and accomplishment at each grade level that is standardized by province or state.

Every child develops at his or her own pace, as I've explained over and over. The same goes for academic skills. Expectations for kindergarten and grade 1 have grown and increased as the years have gone by. It used to be that if a child could recognize some letters, perhaps write his or her name, were at a "pre-reading stage" and had begun to "colour within the lines", they were considered "ready" for kindergarten. It seems that expectations for skill development have increased as the years have gone by, because I've heard from some parents that their children were expected to already be doing some reading on entering kindergarten.

It used to be that kindergarten was for learning how to play with other children, for getting used to being in school and teaching some developmental basics. Grade 1 was the beginning of the academic focus of school, with school becoming full-day after the half-time in kindergarten. Some school systems now run full-day kindergartens all week or with full days spread out through the week on alternating days. That is quite a big change that can have a kindergartener quite tired after a full day at school. For some, the faster pace and longer days can be tough.

Getting into reading at a younger age, in kindergarten instead of grade 1 can be tough on some children, as well. Although some children have always naturally been reading before they started school, some haven't been ready and this can cause some upset, frustration and distress for them and their parents. Going from recognizing some letters to recognizing words to knowing what letters "sound like" and sounding them out to make words is a huge leap. Every step is a big accomplishment and every child will "get it" at their own pace.

What if your child isn't progressing as fast as the rest of the class? Try and work with the teacher to get some help in exercises to encourage these skills at home. Patience is the watch-word with acquiring any new skill, and if working at home causes frustration and upset, maybe take turns as parents when the going gets tough…tag-teaming with each other can give each of you a break and a fresh energy to each study attempt. There are also some marvellous computer learning games out there now that can help your child work on these skills while having fun at the same time. They can be very helpful, as well. Don't forget grandparents and other extended family…if your child is close to them and they seem to have more patience than you, ask if they'd be willing to help.

What if, despite all of yours and the teacher's efforts, your child is still struggling? A referral for an assessment by the school resource person or school psychologist can help pin-point where they are having difficulty. If the teacher suggests it, listen to them. You have nothing to lose and an opportunity to understand what is happening for your child better. It is nothing to worry about, but gives you all the more information to better understand where your child may be having difficulty. They can give suggestions to work on any areas that need help both at home and at school. There are also some terrific resources out there of private tutoring programs and facilities that cater to helping children in various areas and they may be an added resource.

The most important thing to remember is that your child needs and craves success experiences. Remember to focus on cheering on their strengths and every effort they make to work on areas that require more growth. A child who feels like a "failure" in school at any grade does not go on to expect success in later grades. Every one counts towards their later success in life.

Social Expectations:

What if your child doesn't seem to be getting along with others in the classroom? Remember, school is as much a social as an academic experience. Feeling good about themselves socially is as important as academically. A child who feels alone or like a "black sheep" in the classroom can really start to not enjoy school. Friendships build on each other from year to year and although new kids come into the classroom throughout the year and at each new grade, making sure that your child has the social skills to make friends is something that you've been working on since well before they entered school.

Again, working with the teacher to find out who your child associates and gets along with can help for you to encourage these friendships outside of the classroom. If there is a child they have problems with, try and work with the teacher to make things better and perhaps approach the child's parents to work with you. Encouraging your child to be assertive and seek help if problems arise by talking to the teacher or playground supervisor can help them learn to deal with situations.

If making friends is still hard for your child, practice the skills needed to interact with and make friends at home or at a local park. What comes naturally for some takes time for others. All it has to begin with is learning to say "Hello, my name is…What's your name? Do you want to play?" and each success experience makes your child feel more confident to keep on trying. You can practice this with your child at home, role-playing each part so that they feel comfortable with approaching another child to play. Cheer them on with their efforts and remind them of successes they've had. For some children, at least having friends at other activities or on sports teams can make a big difference in their self-esteem.

Your Child's Teacher:

You and your child's teacher are a team working together to help your child. What if he or she doesn't seem to be listening to your concerns? What if they can't seem to find the time to meet or deal with any concerns or issues you may have? Remember that there will always be personality differences between people and sometimes, no matter how hard you try, it sometimes doesn't seem to be working. If meeting in person isn't productive or can't be arranged, try writing a note to the teacher with your concerns and suggest a time to meet. If you still find your concerns aren't being addressed, it may be time to talk to the school principal.

Every parent has the right and responsibility to advocate for their child. As we know from the business world, if we don't get satisfaction at one level, we sometimes need to work our way up. Although it may feel like "tattling" or that you're going above their head (you are!), you must do what you think is best for your child. Of course, no one wants bad feelings to interfere in working with someone, but if the situation isn't workable, sometimes you may have to have the principal mediate and monitor your concerns. They may be able to help alleviate any misunderstandings or miscommunication that have gotten in the way. It is, after all in the best interests of your child.

Grade by Grade:

The rule-of-thumb for how the grades progress is that the odd-numbered grades are bigger learning years and the even-numbered grades reinforce and solidify what's been learned the year before. Let's see how this works…Grade 1 is (or used to be) all about learning to read, as it is essential to every learning year after that. Grade 2 strengthens and reinforces that skill for some, gives others the chance to perhaps catch up. Grade 3 is about greater reading comprehension, not just being able to read but to understand what they read. Grade 4 is about strengthening the previous skills. Grade 5 starts spreading reading comprehension to new subjects like Science, Social Studies and Math. Whereas before, math problems were more than likely numbers alone, in grade 5 they become written problems. I'll continue with this developmental progression through the grades later on…

****

The early school years are crucial ones for your child to feel good about themselves both socially and academically. There are so many types of intelligence: academic, social, creative, artistic, musical, kinaesthetic (sports and other physical activities), mechanical, and emotional, to name a few. Remember that no one is a master at or good at everything. The key during these early years is to help your child **want** to learn, to celebrate their successes and try harder at what is more difficult for them. Effort deserves to be rewarded as a success, because persistence when the going gets tough will get them there. Your patience, encouragement and enthusiasm is contagious. We want them to cheer themselves on, to keep on trying and feel good about themselves. There are lots of school years ahead!!!

Chapter 13

Elementary school: Knowing what they need to know and grow

I have already mentioned a few of the expectations for learning at each grade with respect to reading ability. Remember that what your child learns each year builds upon what they learned the year before. Teachers know that children will typically lose some ground between school years with the break off for the summer. That simply comes from lack of practicing academic skills. Just like any skill, lack of practice and exercise of any muscle group can cause it to lose some of its strength and that big 'ol brain muscle is no different!

Think of activities that you don't do on a regular basis: perhaps doing your taxes, as you don't work on them every day. Each year that you begin them, it's kind of like starting over as you try to figure out what you did the year before. A good way to ensure that your child is ready for the next grade is by doing some school exercises over the summer. It doesn't mean sitting down and doing school every day, just some warm-up practices to keep them up with what they've learned.

Another really good practise that you can do all the time is to help make what they learn relevant and useful in daily life. The biggest refrain I hear from kids in junior high and high school is: "When will I ever need to know this?". By using their growing reading and math skills to measure things, read instructions for building things or recipes, it makes it come more naturally for them and will propel them to want to learn more. Talking about world events in the news and starting to read parts of the newspaper brings them up-to-speed on the world around them. It helps them understand the global and mutual impact of where they live on the rest of the world and vice-versa. Keeping up with changes and developments in science and technology is easy, as well. It is a part of our ongoing news coverage.

Engaging your child in learning more about our world helps them want to learn even more, which they will be doing in each and every grade. Touching on the major subject areas (Language Arts, Math, Social Studies and Science) makes what they are learning relevant, useful, and interesting.

Let's not forget about the "optional" or supplementary classes that most children have on their curriculum, as well. Gym or Physical Education, Music and Art are the most popular ones in the early grades, as well as perhaps another language being studied. Luckily, Physical Education has become a standard part of every curriculum because we have all heard and seen that our population, including our children, are becoming heavier, to the point of obesity. There is no substitute for physical activity to help in muscle development, coordination and weight maintenance.

Even if your child doesn't seem to be great at sports, encourage them to try their best nonetheless. Enjoyment of and participation in sports activities is often the best memories many of us have of our childhoods. It can also be some of the worst for some. If a child is consistently not picked for teams until last, hasn't developed the skills yet, he or she likely will lose confidence and not want to play. No one has to be a professional athlete or great at it, but the camaraderie and team-spirit it can help create carries us throughout our lives. If your child needs some practice in some of the basics like running, catching, throwing or kicking a ball, why not get out there and play with them? It's great for you both...

There is so much more to be learned from sports other than the skills in the sport itself. Workplaces frequently work in "teams", which need cooperation, negotiation, leadership, and collaboration, among other skills. Children can learn to be leaders, to cooperate, and work together in sports activities. It's not just about the physical skills. Encourage these social aspects of sports participation, as well, as these lessons will be lifelong for the game of life.

Music classes open up a whole new world for children. Learning to read and play music in itself is like learning a whole new language. Being able to appreciate different types of music, let alone play them, takes us back to the roots of where it all began. Not everyone has a love for every type of music, but if you listen to even the most popular entertainers of today, their musical roots began in the classics or jazz, blues, or old-time country music. Encouraging your child to play first the recorder and other instruments made available to them in school provides them with another source of pride and accomplishment. Not everyone will become a famous musician, but being able to play an instrument for the sheer joy of it is a wonderful skill that will last them through their lives. Encourage them to practice at home and give little "recitals"…even if not with an instrument, then the songs they've learned to sing. If they have a chance, suggest they join the school choir. Choirs always need new members, girls and boys.

Just like Phys Ed and Music classes, Art classes provide another form of creativity and self-expression. Treasure those art projects that your child proudly brings home. They may not be amazing to others, but beauty is in the eye of the beholder. Always encourage your child's artistic endeavours. If you aren't sure what it is that they've made, don't let them know. Let them tell you. Nothing can hurt more than an excited child bringing home a picture of something they drew or painted and their parent says "Great ____!", and it wasn't supposed to be that. Join in their imagination and notice how their skills grow over time. Comment on the colours, the textures, anything you can. Proudly display them on your fridge to show how you appreciate them/

Many schools provide second-language courses or Immersion in other languages. Who can argue that learning another language can be anything but beneficial in our global world? The early childhood years are the easiest time for a person to learn another language. If it's a language you don't know, try your best to learn along with your child, as being able to practice at home is often the best predictor of success. Let them "teach" you and see their pride in knowing more about something than their parents!

For children in Immersion language programs, understand that it is much harder if the language isn't spoken or understood at home. They don't have the same opportunity to practice and get help in homework and this puts them at a distinct disadvantage. If your child is struggling in another language program (and I'm sure you've researched it carefully before enrolling them), understand that all of their subjects are in that language except for English. Learning Math, Social Studies and Science in a different language other than their own can be very difficult and without your ability to help them, they can fall behind. Work closely with their teachers, just like in any school program.

If your child is having a hard time in an Immersion program, talk honestly with their teachers about whether it is the right course of study for them. They may do great in their subjects if it is in English and this is a fine balance you must weigh. A child's self-esteem can be badly damaged by not doing well at school. You must decide whether having high marks in all their subjects at an English-language school with a language option is better for them than perhaps mediocre or poor marks in a course of study in a different language. It doesn't mean that they can't learn the language independently at the same time or later on in life, but perhaps giving them a fighting chance to do well in school is the most important goal.

The importance of "options" cannot be underscored. Some children just don't find as much success academically in their core courses and it can be a source of shame or weakness for them. Self-confidence comes from finding out that you're good at something. Celebrate what your child tries and is good at. After all, a Chopin didn't have to be a mathematical genius and Picasso didn't have to be able to write successful short stories, did he? Remind them that Einstein failed math in school and still ended up being one of the greatest geniuses of the 20th century! They will have leaps and bounds in their development. What was almost impossible the year before may come to them easily the next school year. Build upon what they know, encourage the heck out of their strengths and efforts to overcome their weaker areas.

Not every child's development is even across all areas of growth and development. In fact, for most, it's not. A really gifted and talented child academically may not be socially or emotionally mature for his or her age. A really gifted child athletically may not be functioning at their grade-level academically. A wonderfully social child may not be great at academics or sports, but we help them recognize their strengths and build confidence from them while working on other areas that may not yet be as well developed.

Supplementing your child's school education with extra-curricular activities can only serve to help them in every other area of their lives. I can't tell you the times I interviewed children and youth who were having problems in life, whether with the law, in their families or their social lives. What struck me repeatedly was that many had no sources of self-esteem. When asked if they did well at school, they found limited pleasure or success in it. Socially, many had few friends or were loners. They had never been involved in any outside activities like art classes, music or drama classes or youth groups. They were never involved in any sports other than what they could do on their own. What a sad situation when a child has no place where they can feel good about themselves!

There is a fine balance between involvement and over-involvement, however. We seem to be seeing many children nowadays who have so many outside commitments of sports practices and classes that they have little "down-time" to do their homework, get together with friends or just relax. Relaxation time is important, too, to help recharge their batteries. Having the time to socialize with friends is an important part of their development, as well, even though they may have friends at each of their activities. If a child is up at all hours doing homework past bedtime and is tired for school the next day from a hectic after-school schedule, there is a problem there, as well.

I am a firm believer in opening up your child's world to any activities they might enjoy and find success at. Who knows, your child may be a Gretzky-in-the-making and if they never got that chance to skate and play hockey, no one would ever have known. They may never be expert at golf or a martial art or soccer, gymnastics or softball, skiing, swimming, drama, art or a musical instrument, but by giving them the chance to learn and acquire a skill, they can carry it on and enjoy into their adulthood. Beware becoming too wrapped up in their successes and being too pushy, however. Let them take their time and enjoy it, not to please you. Many parents see their children's interest and enthusiasm wane at outside activities as they get older and this can be sad, because you enjoyed them doing them so much. But what they've learned will stay with them, perhaps to be picked up again at a later time in their lives. What has been learned is never really lost.

Back to School

As I already mentioned in describing the progression of reading skills that build upon each other with each grade, the same goes for mathematical skills. What begins as addition and subtraction moves on to multiplication and division as well as fractions and decimals. Learning each new skill builds upon previous ones. And each of these skill areas (reading and math) feeds into Social Studies and Science. Reading comprehension is critical for reading Social Studies text books. Science requires measurement and an understanding of mathematics. They all build upon and supplement each other.

If your child gets "stuck" or hits a road-block in let's say multiplication, work it through with them using examples from the teacher. Follow their examples, because your children are learning the "new math" and teaching them the way you may have learned may give them the "right" answer, but in showing their work, they have to be able to get it right the "right way". If you can, use real-world examples to pique their interest in a subject that may not interest them. For instance, in a child who may dislike math but loves baseball or hockey, show them how the "stats" of their favourite players or teams are mathematically based. Sometimes, the motivation to learn something needs to be driven by giving it a purpose they can relate to and want to understand.

If your child struggles with reading and isn't motivated, don't be so willing to read them the instructions or information on a video game they enjoy. Help them to try to read it for themselves. If books don't seem to interest them, try magazines in subjects they enjoy. The pictures provide some information, but they are more likely to want to read about the pictures. They may enjoy comic books. Who cares? At least learning to read along with the story lines gets them to practice their skills.

I can't reiterate enough about how crucial reading is to success academically and in life. Imagine if you couldn't read the "fine print" at the bottom of things you sign or the prices of what you buy or the instructions on a bottle of medication. In doing academic assessments of children at all ages, I have so often found them "stuck" at reading levels far below their grade. I seem to remember the 3rd grade seem to be a sticking point from the many assessments I completed. We are talking here about children, often in high school and junior high still stuck at a grade 3 reading level. How can they hope to understand what they have to read in their text-books at these higher grades? Even newspapers are geared to at least a grade 5 reading level!

Education is available to everyone. Doesn't your child deserve to benefit from what is available to them, to learn everything they can, to feel good about themselves and what they've learned? Being involved in your child's education, helping them learn, working with their teachers is a duty we owe to our children. We may not have enjoyed school or had success there, but it's not fair to condemn our children to the same fate. Education is the big equalizer that makes opportunity available to everyone.

With people moving around the world to give their children a better education, opportunities and a better life, we have a responsibility to make our children's education count and help them be competitive. Success in school, whether academic, social, artistic/creative, musical, in school sports or in any combination will propel them to a better life and feeling good about themselves. The biggest predictor of future success for those who "make it" is good self-esteem and believing in themselves. That is the greatest gift, outside of unconditional love, that you can give your child.

Chapter 14

Junior High: The soap opera of life begins…

Junior high begins for some school systems at the grade 6 level, for others at grade 8. Some skip it entirely and go from elementary right to high school at grade 9. In any case, the leap to grade 7 seems to be a big one for many developmental (and hormonal!) reasons. Grade 7 is a big learning year after grade 6 which was to ensure that they have all of the building blocks under their belt that they needed to learn from the elementary years. Add in social issues, pubertal changes and a possible change in schools and you have quite the pre-teen on your hands!!!

Junior high is a big leap in freedom, choices and variety. Feeder schools from smaller elementary schools funnel into bigger junior highs where there are many more kids and the opportunities to meet new friends. It can be a good thing for children to meet more available peers, but also a potential bad one if you don't know the families. Going from an elementary school, often closer to home, to a junior high farther away, children may be more likely to bring their lunches and eat in the lunch-room (if they haven't already). They have more time on their hands to wander after eating lunch, perhaps in the surrounding neighbourhood (if you give them permission).

This is part of the freedom, but so is the choice to choose options outside of what has been available before. Cooking, sewing and industrial arts (carpentry, welding, automotive shop) are often choices available. Many a mechanic, welder, chef or clothing designer first found their passion taking these classes and it starts to open up your child to a world of possibilities.

From the first years in school when your child had one classroom teacher and perhaps a gym or music or art teacher as well, now your child has a multitude of teachers who teach them in each of their classes. They will have a "home room", but will more than likely have an English teacher, a Math teacher, a teacher for Science and Social Studies, as well. Coordinating homework between the various classes can become a challenge, as they may not be in contact with each other and some days may have loads of homework combined between teachers. Dealing with different teachers' personalities, not just one, can become a challenge. It is a great opportunity to better understand their world out there where they must learn to relate to and get along with all different people.

Organization becomes key in figuring out how to navigate and complete work from each teacher. With junior highs being bigger, there is not as much opportunity to prod and direct each child (although many teachers work very hard at it!), and your child will need to become more self-sufficient and self-directed in their work and study habits. Keeping up with their work becomes even more important for a parent to do. With technology today, many teachers post their home-work assignments on-line and this can help you help your child ensure that they're keeping up. With the advent of email technology as well, some teachers graciously provide email addresses to promote contact with parents about their child's progress. Parent-teacher meetings become even more important with so many more people in your child's life.

Now let's look at hormonal changes, the joy of "attitude", the fight for independence and the free spirit...It doesn't have to begin at puberty or junior high anymore, but seems to be developing earlier and earlier. Riding on the wave of media exposure, elementary school kids are as susceptible to what they see as anyone. They want to grow up too fast, to dress much older than their ages, and to do things that we would never have dreamed of doing at their ages. Peer pressure becomes even greater. This is not a new concept. We all felt it in our day, but with other kids doing more and having more freedom, reigning in your child from what everyone else is doing becomes harder.

Puberty

It seems that children are hitting puberty earlier than ever before. Who knows why? It could be the hormones that were in milk (supposedly no longer in there now), better nutrition and hygiene, or any other number of causes. Some girls are starting their periods as early as age 9 or 10 (grade 4 or 5) and the same changes are happening in boys. Of course, preparing your child in advance should be before junior high, because it may happen sooner for them. It is more than an unfair surprise for a girl who is unprepared to suddenly start menstruating at school. I had a friend that had it happen to her and to say it was traumatic is an understatement. Explain to your child that it is a normal stage of development and send her prepared with feminine hygiene items in her backpack. Not every washroom has a dispenser. Being prepared makes everything less scary and more a normal part of life. It also removes the stigma of teasing if it comes as a surprise.

Just as girls start menstruating and developing more body hair, boys develop more hair, develop deeper voices, perhaps start shaving (it's a big comparison with each other, who has to shave first), and start having wet dreams. Please, parents, talk to your boy about it in advance! I have talked to too many youth who, at a later age, had thought they had "wet the bed" and were ashamed and embarrassed about this new development. They guiltily skulked off to wash their sheets and told no one, but it was a scarring experience at the time.

The obvious physical development of greater muscle mass in boys, breasts and greater curves in girls have potentially huge implications for their social lives. A boy who is bigger-muscled earlier has an advantage in sports and it can be a huge source of self-esteem for them. It can increase their popularity immensely and make them more appealing to friends and possible girlfriends. A boy who develops later may be at a social disadvantage in sports and with their peers, not seen as "mature" as the boys who develop earlier.

A girl who develops sooner can become more appealing to the boys and envied by the girls, but it can rush her social life into dating sooner. If she is perceived as more sexually appealing earlier than the other girls, it may incur some jealousy in the girls and get in the way of just plain friendships with boys. I remember talking to a peer in high school who had developed early and she reiterated how it had pushed her into dating earlier, as the boys saw her as dating material, whereas she had just wanted to be friends. It can even have a negative impact on sports success with girls, as they negotiate running and jumping with the added bounce and weight of their breasts to get used to.

Friends

We were the centre of our children's universe when they were little and slowly as they get older, their friends become more and more important to them. They are more likely to talk to friends about what's going on for them, what's bothering them than they are to you. That's expected but sad at the same time. The best we can do is provide them with healthy, pro-social activities and groups with similar interests outside of school, but again, we have no control over who they meet and socialize with at school.

Pre-teens and teens are "pack animals" who will tend to follow in order to fit in as they become more self-conscious. There is always a leader-of-the-pack, however, and helping your child to be a leader is extremely important. Leadership skills involve good self-esteem, self-confidence and good social skills, among other traits. It is nurtured from a young age by parents who have been responsive and involved with their children, helping them feel good about themselves both at school, at home, and in other activities. A child who feels poorly about themselves can be at a distinct disadvantage socially, leaving them more open to outside influences.

Try to remain involved in and aware of your child's social life, the friendships they choose, and nurture or encourage the "good ones". Get to know other parents so that you can keep in touch with each other about what you or they may see happening. If you have issues with new friends you don't know, invite your child to have them over for dinner so that you can get to know them. Remember that if there is a friend you don't care for, voicing your concerns can have several possible effects: it may discourage the friendship and your child will focus elsewhere, or it may actually encourage the friendship, in defiance of what you think. Remember Romeo and Juliet? Yes, it can happen with friendships, as well as romantic interests. If your child persists with the friendship, the best you can do is to try to get to know the child, which allows you to monitor things a bit. What you don't want is a friendship to persist behind your back, as sneakiness can lead to other things…

All of us know that children can be incredibly kind and incredibly mean, as well. We have all seen the teen movies about the misery children can be put through by the "popular kids". It is devastating to their self-esteem and they need your help. If they have friends outside of school, strengthen and encourage those relationships so that your child has a source of social belonging elsewhere. Encourage your child to be assertive, rebuffing the teasing or ignoring it. Sometimes this works and they actually earn respect for standing up for themselves, but sometimes it makes things worse. We can't predict which way it will go, and if things persist to make your child's school life a horror story, engage the help of the teachers. Being considered a "tattle-tale" is always a possible consequence, but teachers know how to watch for and catch situations, to encourage a child who needs a little help socially to find some positive support in their peers. Remember that teachers are there to help encourage children's development not just academically, but also emotionally and socially. A sympathetic teacher or coach can make all the difference in the world.

I have often noted that when boys don't get along, they seem to get over it faster to become friends again. They just seem to be able to shake it off, get out there and do things together again, the disagreement forgotten. It seems to be different with girls, who seem to hold grudges for longer. The flip-flop between "best friends" and "greatest enemies" seems to happen a lot with girls, who tend to be more forthcoming with each other (and hence, have more "ammunition" to hurt each other). Losing a best friend can be devastating, as they have probably shared so much with each other. Encouraging other friendships, or perhaps bringing them together to talk about making things better can help. Understand that it is a huge loss for a child to lose a friend.

Alcohol, drugs and smoking:

A familiar refrain from parents becomes: "Just because other kids do it, because other parents let them doesn't mean we have to let you!" and the fight begins…It's not new, we heard it and argued for greater freedom and autonomy, but there seem to be so many more dangers out there in today's world. We can only hope that we have taught our children to keep themselves safe and make good choices with everything that is available to them. Under-aged drinking (don't be naïve, it can happen even in the elementary years!) can happen at parties. They may not be of age to buy it, but can have older kids "boot" it for them for a price. And then there's drugs…

Of course, drugs have been available for millennia. Opium was the drug-of-choice hundreds of years ago, morphine was used as a calming agent in previous centuries, cocaine was used for medication and coca leaves were used for thousands of years by indigenous peoples in South America to help with dealing with working at high altitudes. Peyote, hallucinogenic mushrooms has similarly been used for religious/spiritual purposes by indigenous peoples for aeons. What I'm talking about here is the easy availability of street drugs, chemicals that have been created to "hook" people. Even the relatively "soft" drugs like marijuana have been "cut" with additional ingredients like crack or other chemicals that are addictive and dangerous. It seems like we're always hearing about some new drug out there with new dangers that is catching on. Even despite all of the warnings and inevitable deaths from them, that doesn't stop others from taking a chance and trying them.

Of course, there is more public education on television and in schools to educate and deter your child from trying and using drugs. However, they are readily available, often sold inside or just outside school-yards. They have a ready market eager to try, with a greater disposable income. Peer pressure to "just try it" is strong and sometimes, the "cool kids" are the ones who are more adventurous. What can you do?

I really believe that having your child involved in extra-curricular groups and sports where they have peers with similar interests and keep busy with activities is very important during this transition and beyond. Success in sports, outside activities and social groups leads to higher self-esteem and less need to "fit in". Greater assertiveness to not allow themselves to be pushed into trying things they know are not good for them comes from feeling good about themselves. A passive, lonely child is ripe-for-the-picking to be recruited into groups who don't have success or "fit in", themselves.

Keep the communication open with your pre-teen/teenager and talk about what's going on in their lives. If you don't know, ask! If they know you're interested and care, they will be more likely to share what's going on in their lives. Monitor their money, any changes in behaviour or attitude. If you see changes that you can't explain, ask friends' parents if they know what's going on. Ask teachers, coaches and care-givers to keep you up on what they see happening. Don't be shocked if your child tells you they've been offered drugs or alcohol. The fact that they're telling you is a good sign because they resisted the temptation. Be proud of them for making good choices and reinforce that you know it is out there.

If you suspect your child is using or has tried drugs or alcohol, don't be accusatory. Be calm and invite them to talk about it. No one is going to admit to something they know will cause more trouble, but if they know they can talk to you they will be more likely to open up. If you need extra help explaining or working it through, perhaps have another family member join in the discussion with their experiences. If things get out-of-hand, seek professional help. There are some really good public drug and alcohol treatment programs out there who can provide information, do an assessment and help talk to your child. Pretending it isn't happening doesn't help anyone.

What if you find out your child is smoking? It's not a good thing to find out, but at least it's not drugs (although it is a drug, itself and illegal for minors to buy)! Again, try to be calm and not accusatory. You have every right to prevent them from smoking in the house and yard and that's a good course of action, but understand there are many other places they can go to smoke. Perhaps a trip to the family doctor can help, as they provide information about the long-term and short-term health hazards of smoking on health and development.

The opposite sex and dating

Of course, we have encouraged our children to have friendships with the opposite sex, as it takes away the mystery and provides them with more possible friends. Junior high used to signal the beginning of possible "dating" with the inevitable hormones racing. Unfortunately from my perspective, "dating", or "hanging out" seems to be starting earlier in children nowadays, in the elementary school years.

Hopefully, you've already had "the talk" about sex. Not talking about it doesn't mean it isn't going to happen. Being an ostrich with your head buried in the sand only leads to possible surprises. When you talk to your child about safe sex, the possibility of pregnancy and communicable diseases, it isn't giving them permission. It is giving them greater knowledge to make better choices. Your religious beliefs may practice abstinence, celibacy and no sex before marriage, but the media and peers provide different messages. Unwanted pregnancy, herpes and other sexually transmitted diseases are rampant today in the young…better with education, of course, but still out there. Letting them know that it isn't just intercourse that can infect them is just the beginning, but useful information, nonetheless. Many a youth has gotten a life-long STD still being a virgin, never having had intercourse.

Sometimes, group "dates" or going out to the movies in a group is a safe beginning. That way, they're not alone and have the support of friends to socialize with and protect them. Just because you proclaim "no dating until you're 16!" doesn't mean they're going to listen. They may, or they may "hang out" together without your knowledge. What goes on in secret is always possibly a danger. Keep the lines of communication open. Encourage honesty and it will be rewarded by your child being more open. If you discourage it by yelling, accusing or blaming, they may be more likely to keep it hidden. The more you know, the better.

<u>Babysitting, jobs & allowance</u>

Some children begin babysitting for extra pocket money once they're old enough to take babysitting courses at about age 12. It is a great source of self-esteem and pride, feeling trusted to take care of someone's children and good practice for parenting in later life. Some children may begin working in the family business or at paper routes to earn extra money. It is always a fine balance between this added responsibility and letting them just "be kids". You obviously don't want your child working too much that it affects their schooling or social life.

Some parents don't want their children to work while they're in school, feeling that they will spend enough time in the work-force later in life. Your child will increasingly want some pocket money to buy him- or herself extra treats or special things. You may have already instituted an allowance for them to earn with chores at home. It's a great idea, for them to learn the value of money and work, how to save and feel good about themselves when they have worked hard for something they really want.

Teaching your child to budget, start and keep up with a bank account, watching their money "grow" can be a very rewarding learning experience that prepares them for the future. Access to more money can also lead to other temptations, however. Children today have access to drugs, alcohol and cigarettes with more money. Like everything else, it is a fine balance. Just because they don't have access to money from you or a job doesn't mean there aren't other ways to make it. Teach them to work for it, whether at home with chores or odd-jobs or outside jobs. What they've saved and worked towards will be even more of a source of pride and self-esteem. I bought my first car with the money I had saved from working since I was 14 years old and I know that I babied that little '78 Corolla far more than my peers who were given cars by their parents.

Driving

Further along the road towards greater freedom, in some provinces and states, children (or youth) can achieve their Beginner's or Learner's Permit to drive with the supervision of an adult driver at age 14. As unbelievable as it may seem, some kids are driving before they can shave or even have a period. It is a huge milestone for someone to obtain their Learner's and a tremendous source of pride. They will compare with each other who got it first, how many times it took to pass the written exam, who "gets to" drive with their parents more often. You may or may not be thrilled with your child getting a License or Permit at this age, but it is important to them.

If you can and your temperament can handle it, take them out for practices in safe places with little traffic (like a community centre parking lot that isn't busy or a parking lot that isn't busy on the weekend). Isn't it better if you can see how they drive and you can teach them good habits? Of course, driving lessons from an approved, licensed driving school will help ensure that they have the latest rules and regulations in place (and that will happen the closer they get to be able to get a graduated license around 16), but sharing this experience with your child shows them that you are excited to be a part of each stage of their development.

Just as for adults, it goes without saying that drinking and driving are a recipe for disaster. If they're out with friends, encourage them to be the "DD" (designated driver). If they've been drinking, encourage them to call you to pick them up. Even if they're not the driver, encourage them to call you to pick them up. Being awakened by a call from a teen who has had too much to drink and wants a ride home is far better than a call from the police with terrible news.

A word here about cell-phones and driving...and it applies to adults as much as it does to teens. There is a reason that insurance rates for younger drivers is so high, because they are the most likely to get into accidents. Deaths from car accidents are the highest in young people. They can be impulsive, have a sense of immortality, and they almost all have cell-phones. Despite laws everywhere against it, people still drive while texting and talking on their cell-phones. Driving takes focus and attention. Driving while using a cell-phone is distracted driving. Enough said.

****

The joy of seeing your child achieve teenage-hood signals the end of childhood as we know it, but don't let that kid within them and you be ignored or forgotten. They are still the children you knew, only bigger and perhaps wiser or more experienced in the world. It doesn't mean you can't still play and do things together, laugh together and enjoy many of the same things. Don't assume they won't still enjoy some of the same things they did when they were younger. Make it playful and keep close. After all, isn't there still just a big kid inside each of us?

Chapter 15
High School: Helping to ensure good experiences, growth & maturity

The transition to high school entails even more freedom and need for self-directed study. Just as for the transition from elementary school to junior high, a high school combines students from any number of junior high feeder schools, providing new opportunities for your teenager to meet and make new friends. With larger classrooms, even more optional classes available and thus more teachers, it becomes very much more an individual effort to succeed. Teachers are even less likely to be able to chase down a student with a missing assignment and it falls on your teen (and you, if you can), to keep up.

With new technology as already mentioned, many teachers post assignments and exam schedules on the school website. It helps students to stay organized, keep up and remember important dates. Helping your teenager juggle homework assignments and exams, at least in the beginning of high school can give them a distinct advantage because it can be overwhelming.

Before they even find or get to their new classrooms, the sheer size of high schools can be overwhelming and scary for a newcomer. If you can, try to get an orientation visit to their new school with your teen before school starts. Some junior high schools schedule them near the end of the last junior high term. It always helps to familiarize ourselves with a new and strange place. Taking away some of the fear of the unknown by at least knowing where the office and gym are, even having a map of the school in advance can alleviate some of the jitters.

It's not just the new place that can create anxiety, it's the new people. Hopefully, your teen has other friends from their previous school who are attending their new school with them. They may even meet friends from elementary school who went off to different junior highs that are feeder schools into the same high school. Encourage them to stick together in those first few days, so that being a newcomer doesn't feel so alone. Help them understand that just like when they went to junior high for the first time (if they did go to one), it takes time to adjust but they will feel less lost and more a part of things just like they did before. Sharing the experience with other new-comers is a big source of support.

For teens who may not have felt very happy socially in school before, a new school is a new beginning. Encourage your teen to have a fresh start, to be the person they want to be and to meet new friends. It takes a lot of guts to put a brave face forward, but sometimes the loneliness of past school years can be erased with new and different friendships. Encourage them to join clubs, teams and groups where they can meet teens with similar interests.

With the greater variety of optional classes available, high school students have more opportunities to find things that they like doing and feel confident about. It allows them to stretch their interests and find new activities that they may enjoy. Joining into the school spirit with activities and clubs also makes them feel less alone and more a part of things.

Students began being streamed into more individualized academic programs near the end of junior high. What this means is that there are different levels for each core subject, according to a student's perceived capability. Remember that few people are good at every subject and they may be in higher levels in some than others. This can be a source of disappointment or upset for some, who want to achieve higher level courses for college and university entrance. You can help by working with academic advisors to plan out options available for them. Sometimes outside resources or teachers are available to help them achieve their goals to move up to the next level class.

Some students are not academically inclined or they may be more interested already in careers they learn about in optional courses. Trade programs can start at the early stages of high school, sometimes giving your teen the advantage of earning credit towards or a completed internship or apprenticeship. Work-study programs in their chosen field can also provide work experience and high school credits.

Explore along with your teen as they try to figure out what they may want to do as a career. Be open and listen…don't preach or push your point of view. They need to be invested in and willing to put the time and effort into training in whatever field they choose. Fields that they explore will not necessarily become their eventual career, but give them the freedom to imagine and understand what each would entail. Many (of us, too!) have been pushed into career directions that do not suit them or they lose interest in and end up changing careers mid-stream. It is important for the internal drive and interest to be there…maybe not right now, but in the future.

Don't expect your teen to necessarily know what they want to do by the end of high school. Some are just focused on getting through it and graduating (hopefully!). What if your teen is not motivated or interested in school or any activities there? Hopefully, they will still be involved in some extra-curricular activities that provide a source of belonging and self-esteem. Meeting with teachers is always an important part of your child's academic success and they can help. Perhaps your child needs extra encouragement or attention from a teacher to engage them in a subject. Meeting with the teacher and your teen can help them see that they're there to help.

Personality differences, just like in any relationship, can impact on anyone's performance. I can remember having a teacher in high school who I was sure didn't like me and I felt picked-on when asked to do written applied math problems on the board in front of everyone. When my parents were going to parent-teachers for the first time, I told them how ostracized I felt and they talked with that teacher with interest, finding out that he actually really liked having me in the class and saw me as needing more confidence in the subject. He was surprised at how I felt in response to his efforts and when my parents told me what he had said, it made a huge difference for me. He became one of my favourite teachers and my confidence in the class grew immensely. It was a learning experience for us both.

I had occasion to do such an "intervention" with one of my son's and one of my daughter's teachers. They had felt that they were "picked-on" or singled out in both cases and in each one, working with the teachers, we were able to help each of them succeed and feel better about the teacher and class. When a teacher sees that a parent is concerned and involved with helping their child succeed, how can they not want to better understand and help that child? In speaking with teachers through the years both as a school resource and as a parent, they often noted to me how sad it was that often the parents who attended parent-teacher's meetings were the ones whose children were doing fine and the ones who weren't often didn't attend. How can your child have a team working with and for them if they don't meet and work together?

Parent-Teen Relationships

Your child has probably reached teen-hood before attending high school, but the greater striving for autonomy and independence becomes stronger and more focused by this time. Teens struggle with the "nagging" (just like we did!) of parents trying to keep them focused on their future success. We want them to be mature enough to work towards the future, deferring immediate gratification in the "now" for rewards and successes in the future.

Unfortunately, with the greater availability of so much, so many things and experiences compared to when we were young, it is sometimes harder for them to set their sights on the future. Even the role-models around them seem to do it…no savings? Take out a loan...no money to buy a car? Lease it...can't afford a vacation this year? Put it on credit...everyone wants everything now. Our consumer-driven economy and marketers target the young who may have more disposable income with still living at home. Teens, like adults, may focus more on jobs to earn the money to get things now instead of working hard at school to achieve more in the future.

We may end up in a head-on battle with teens about concerns for their health, about their education, about their relationships and their future in general. Where does it come from? It comes from our own experiences, the mistakes we may have made, the choices we might have made that impacted on our own lives. I have found that when I talk to teens about this, they are amazed to realize that parents are not trying to control them but to give them choices and control over their own lives instead of making the same mistakes they did.

Parents of teenagers are going through their own developmental stage of aging, maturity and questioning. We have more grey hair and wrinkles showing (welcome to being parents!) and may be starting to have health concerns. We may or not be in careers or jobs that we enjoy and may or may not wish we had taken another path. Some feel trapped in a job because of the economic pressures of keeping up pay-cheque to pay-cheque. We may or may not still be married to the other parent and some may have separated and/or divorced, perhaps having remarried. All of these changes that are happening or have happened impact on parents' concerns for their teens as they approach adulthood. We want them to make the right choices, not take the wrong road.

What do parents argue about with their teens? They argue about staying out late or not coming home, getting too serious too fast in relationships, and about not focusing on school achievement, among a host of many other concerns. Explaining to a teenager that it isn't a power struggle that is the issue about staying out, but their health and safety you are worried about takes away the adversarial nature. Parents of teens are starting to feel the pressures and effects of aging on their own health and want to ensure that their teens stay safe and healthy for their future.

When it comes to romantic relationships, some teens nowadays seem to move very fast into entwined relationships almost like marriage. They may see each other at school, spend time together before and after school and on weekends, talk or text on cell-phones well into the night and at every other activity. I am certainly "dating" myself, but I can well remember the excitement of going on a date once a week and the anticipation of perhaps a few phone calls in-between. We savoured getting to know each other and were in no rush...but things are very different today.

Seeing your teen's life revolve around a boy- or girl-friend instead of school can be infuriating and worrisome. Yes, everyone deserves a social life, but at the expense of their future? A caution about the Romeo and Juliet scenario, however...sometimes, the more you may try to pull them apart, the closer they glue themselves together. Talking to your teen about their relationship, do not try and minimize their feelings. What we heard trivialized as "puppy love" when we were younger felt denigrating and disrespectful. No one can judge or imagine how they feel. A good approach is to explain your concerns about the future, that focusing all their energy on a relationship they may outgrow (not in a childish way, but in developing different interests over time) may leave them lost in other areas of their lives. Oftentimes, friendships get lost-in-the-shuffle as buddies are pushed aside for the new boy-friend/girl-friend. This is hurtful to their friends and for them if the relationship ends and they need the support of those same friends. Patiently talking through your concerns and listening to your teen's perspective avoids the blaming, angry, conflictual stance that can lead to greater defiance.

Concerns with your teen not putting effort into school brings up parents' own educational, vocational and employment history. If you love what you do, you want your teen to be successful at what they choose as a career and that means being successful at school or at least graduating. If you wish you'd made different career choices, had worked harder at school or taken a different further course of study, you don't want your teen to make the same mistakes. The world is even more competitive out there now and we know that those who try hard are more likely to rise to the top and succeed. Talking about your worries and concern for your teen's future path in the reality of today's world can only help them to understand better where you are coming from.

It is important to relate to your teen that you are trying to provide **guidance**, not to control them. They already know the rules, the expectations and laws at home and in life. You taught them and they learned them when they were little. They know what is expected of them and sometimes want to do it their own way. If it doesn't work, resist the temptation to say "I told you so"…they know it for themselves. Sometimes letting them make their own mistakes is a better (though sometimes costly) way for them to see that. Rubbing it in their face can be disrespectful and shaming.

No one learns best through shame and guilt. Try to problem-solve together different options and ways to do things. Make it as positive an experience as possible. If things get heated, take a break. Nothing gets accomplished with yelling on either side as no one listens. Just like for a couple, sometimes writing a note or an email gives the time and distance to get your or their point across without it being dismissed. Give each other the respect of really listening without jumping in.

Learning to relate to your teen helps in your relationship with them in the future and in their future relationships with teachers, bosses, spouses and their own children. Don't you want a positive legacy for yourselves in the future?

****

Remember that the teen years are ones of invulnerability and feelings of immortality. They feel (and we felt) that they have forever, that nothing bad will happen and everything will turn out alright. We know the reality of life…that it doesn't always turn out the way we wanted it to, just like our parents knew it in their day. Understand where they are coming from and help them understand your perspective. Help them see that being there to provide guidance is not an attempt to control them.

Communication, honesty and mutual respect and trust are always the keys to a healthy relationship.

Be honest about how you feel, what you think and why with your teen. Accord them the same respect to hear them out. You may not agree, but give them the respect of listening.

Try to build trust with your teen. If they falter, give them a chance to regain it. Everyone makes mistakes, after all. Let them know that if they make a mistake, it's better to be honest about it rather than keeping it a secret or hidden. It shows integrity and it's easier to accept a mistake when someone owns up to it.

Respect your teen's privacy and space, as these seem to be important to them from what many have told me through the years. Expect and deserve the same respect from them. As parents, we feel disrespected when they argue, yell, name-call or swear. Lead by example and don't do it, either. After all, we weren't too thrilled with the "do as I say, don't do as I do" philosophy of our parents before us.

Be willing to say you were wrong or are sorry. No one is always right and who can help but respect someone more when they admit to being wrong or are sorry?

Above all, keep on talking and listening to your teen. Keep those lines of communication open! Don't let conflict come between you to push you far apart. He or she will always be your child and you will always be their parent. The relationship changes over time and we may not always like each other but will always love each other. Make sure they know that. Our love and belief in them is the cushion and the step that will propel our children into the challenges of the outside world. They need to be able to count on it because it's tough out there...

Chapter 16
If You Have Concerns About Your Child or Teen…

I'm not talking about this just because I'm a psychologist, but because it's important to talk about it. You know your child, have since even before he or she was born. You've seen him or her develop through the years and it's not always an easy road. If you see changes in your child's physical health, you talk to your family physician. If you see changes in your child's academic achievement, you talk to teachers. If you see changes in your child's emotional health, talk to him or her. Those lines of communication you've so carefully cultivated are there for a reason, to be there for them to talk to and share. If you're getting nowhere, still talk to your doctor, teachers, coaches, their friends, anyone who might be able to shed some light on what is happening.

We're talking here about changes in behavior, perhaps a normally outgoing child becomes quiet and reclusive. Perhaps a normally cautious child suddenly becomes careless, inattentive and gregarious. Sometimes, there are things happening for a child or teenager that they haven't been able to share with anyone. These changes in behavior suggest that something has changed in or for them. Don't just ignore it and hope they will go back to themselves. These can be warning signs that they need help.

Bad things can happen to people at all ages. It can happen to those they care about, like the death of a loved one or a parental divorce. It can come from others with bullying or sexual abuse. It can come from themselves, with self-doubt creeping in or a loss of self-confidence. None of us is immune to any of it, but younger people often don't have the internal resources to deal with situations. They may also not be willing to ask for help, possibly out of shame or guilt for how they feel.

Think about it: if a parent or family is struggling in the aftermath of the death of a loved one or is in the middle of a nasty divorce battle, is a child or teen necessarily going to want to add to the burden of what everyone is already going through? If your child shows a muted reaction to situations, it may be because they don't want to worry you even more.

It is so important to be able to talk about your feelings with your child (at an age-appropriate level), but not to burden them with them. In other words, your child or teen is not your confidante, but at the same time, they need to see you deal with your feelings in healthy ways. You are a role-model, their very first! Show them and explain to them how you work through your emotions and experiences.

Often, a child or teen may feel more comfortable talking to one parent or the other. Sometimes, they're most comfortable with a close aunt or uncle or an older sibling. Enlist their help and they'll be more than willing, because they care. All it takes is just one person to help a child or teen unburden themselves of whatever is bothering them.

If they won't or can't seem to talk to anyone in the family and you can't get any information from other people in his or her life (like teachers, coaches, friends), it's time to call in professional help. Parents are much more likely to ask for help when their child or teen is acting out or getting trouble (we call it externalizing) than when the behavior is just the opposite (internalizing). It's just like children with ADHD: the hyperactive, impulsive ones are almost always identified first while often, the inattentive, quiet ones are frequently recognized much later. Ironically, sometimes the child or teen who withdraws is often the one who is more troubled.

A withdrawn child who didn't used to be is telling us something without saying anything...he or she is troubled. If whatever is troubling them is not discussed, it can most certainly fester over time. Not reaching out to the world and those who love him or her makes his or her world much smaller, lonelier and sadder. It used to be thought that children couldn't be depressed, but now we know that it can and does happen. Mental health professionals know that and those specializing in working with children can help. They know how to relate to younger people, to help them feel comfortable with unburdening whatever is troubling them. Sometimes, it's actually easier for a child or teen to share with a professional, because they don't have to worry about hurting anyone's feelings in telling.

I'm belaboring all of this because it's important. Untreated, children who are sad or withdrawn don't necessarily "snap out of it". They don't have the life experience or perspective to know that life will get better. They need help and don't always know who or how to ask for it.

Just as I've talked about the "internalizing" child or teen, those who act out (or "externalize") also need help. Their behavior is telling you something, as they're getting attention in the wrong ways. Children crave positive attention and praise, so if they're not getting it, they'll do whatever it takes to get any attention. Just ask any "class clown"…he (or she) will tell you that they used to act up in class to get attention from their peers many times because they were having academic difficulties or problems at home or conflict with their teachers. Any attention is at least some attention. Children who act out are showing that they need help, more openly than their quiet, withdrawn counter-parts. Their behavior isn't telling what is troubling them, but they're showing it.

Many parents, when disciplining a child who has been acing out will ask them "Why?", "Why are you doing that?". Wrong question. Often, they don't even know why and all this leads to is more frustration on both your parts. Again, ask those who know your child well. They may know of something that is happening or has happened. If no one can tell you why and you don't know, it's time to contact a mental health professional. Acting-out behaviors can and will escalate, starting with little things and then getting bigger.

Now let's look at parent-child relationships. They may be great when the child is younger, but sometimes with a growing need for autonomy and independence, they become more conflictual in the teenage years. I've already talked about ways of relating to your teen that you're not trying to control them, but to help guide them. The idea is that as children mature, they develop self-control so that we don't need to be there to control them.

Very few of us have agreed with every rule set in place by our parents when we were growing up. We've pushed the limits, stretching our wings, insisting that it's a different world we live in from the one our parents grew up in years before. Remember that self-defence? Well, it goes on as the generations continue. You'll probably hear from your children like your parents probably heard it from you and your grand-parents probably heard from them. Nevertheless, we know that in the end, our parents were right to be cautious. But we know that from experience. We didn't know it at the time.

If there's a lot of conflict in your relationship with your child or teen, try tagging out and letting the other parent take a turn. Sometimes, you just need a breather from each other, when emotions aren't so heightened. Sometimes, simply writing notes or emails to each other can give you and your child or teen that needed distance to get your points across. The advantage of this is that it gives whoever is writing about how they feel or what happened a chance to be "heard" without being interrupted, frustrated, and blamed. It is much easier to get a point across when no one is interrupting or talking over you. It's called respect, and should be mutual in any relationship.

So what if you've tried everything you can to relate to your child or teen and every interaction seems to be a battle? Time to see a mental health professional, who will be able to hear both sides objectively and see the dynamics of the relationship. He or she will help you both feel heard, to understand what the other wants and needs, and to learn to relate to each other even better. It's not an overnight fix, but it is a step in the right direction, showing your child or teen how much you care about them and your relationship with them.

Chapter 17
Through it all: Taking care of yourselves as a couple

Parenting doesn't end with children graduating from high school or moving out and getting a job. It is a wonderful, lifelong, life-changing experience for a couple. As you've seen, being "mom" and "dad" adds so much to who we are as people and as a couple. It makes us grow and mature, having to juggle our time and focus on being totally responsible for another human being. At the same time, being parents shouldn't take anything away from being a couple...it should make it even better despite the added stress, frustrations and complications of being parents, as well. It is a partnership, a cushion of support, of mutual caring and cheering. Having shared the experience of raising, nurturing and enjoying your children (as well as the grey hairs!), you have accomplished something wonderful together.

Now what? It goes without saying that being a parent changes our lives forever. It gives a couple even more in common, a dedicated project to nurture and grow together. They are still a couple, however changed from when they first met. When we initially explored whether a couple were ready to start a family, I stressed the importance of still trying to do things together as a couple without the kids as well as supporting each other to maintain individual activities and interests.

Maintaining an identity as an individual helps anyone maintain a sense of themselves as a person in their own right. It makes a couple even stronger, with two people who can enjoy being part of the "team", sharing goals, hopes and dreams, but also who are still individuals in their own right. As parents working together for the family, it can get a little cramped for time trying to maintain yourselves as a couple and as individuals, but all of the effort is well worth it as your children grow older and move on to their own lives.

No couple is the same when they've had children. No person is the same when they've become part of a couple. The experiences together as a couple and as parents enrich our lives and help us to "grow" as people. It makes us less self-centred, less "selfish", but at the same time there is the fine balance of losing yourselves as people and as a couple. There is nothing wrong with doing things for yourself and each other outside of the family. People who have been totally self-sacrificing for the family may have done so for the "greater good" and everyone else may have benefited, but selflessness in the long-run can lead to bitterness and feeling lost when the kids grow up.

Now let's look at it from the children's viewpoint: parents are the ultimate role-models. If you don't do things for yourself, respect yourself by meeting your own needs, what message does that give your children? That you aren't important as a person, that you don't deserve respect because you don't even show yourself respect. When children see parents doing things for themselves, going out with friends, having hobbies and interests apart from being parents, it is a good thing. They come to realize that you are not "just a parent", but a person in your own right. A more fulfilled person is a happier parent. A stressed-out, overwhelmed parent who neglects his or her needs is not going to be a happy person. That angst, self-neglect and growing resentment can't help but spill over onto the children. Do yourself and your children a favor...take care of you! Remember the instructions we're given on an airplane when it comes to using the drop-down air-mask? Use it on yourself first, because you're no help to the other person if you put theirs on first...the same goes to parenting.

How about parents' relationships from the children's point of view? Again, your relationship is their first role-model. Make it a good one. Let them see you being a couple, doing things together, going out on dates. Let them see you nurture each other, love each other, as your love is what brought them into this world. You are a couple, apart from being parents, just as you are individuals apart from being a couple. Show your children your respect for each other, how you communicate, that you are a team. They need to see that "mom and dad" are also "husband and wife".

I have this vision of "empty nesters" sitting at the breakfast table in the morning after the last child has moved away and having nothing to say to each other outside of being "dad" and "mom". No one can continue to live vicariously through their children, their exploits, relationships and accomplishments. What happened to the individuals each person used to be? What happened to the couple they were? It becomes difficult trying to suddenly fill in those gaps when years have gone by apart from doing what they used to enjoy together and on their own, with friends and the world moving on.

As I mentioned, children love to see their parents get dressed up and go out on "dates" together. It reminds them that their parents are adults, apart from being parents, in their own right. "Mom's-" or "Dad's-night-out" also gives them time to spend with the other parent, establishing their own little traditions together. It may be pizza ordered-in while they watch movies, fast-food out and to the nearby park, a favourite meal cooked together and then playing in the backyard, but all are memories that help a child strengthen and enjoy their relationship with each parent. At the same time, it gives the other parent the freedom to socialize on her or his own and still do the activities they enjoy.

Couples often learn to join in and enjoy each other's passions. Many a wife has taken golf lessons to be able to play with her husband or has taken up fishing. Many a husband has taken to cooking along with his wife when he never showed an interest in it before or throws himself wholeheartedly into remodelling their home together. I am being stereotypical here, of course...but you get the idea. Knowing that your spouse loves to do something and joining in often becomes even more fun. It may never be something that is your favourite thing to do or that you are particularly adept at, but doing it together makes it all the better!

Giving each other the freedom to enjoy friendships and activities apart from each other strengthens a couple, as well. There are limits, of course, with husbands and wives who bemoan their spouse being too preoccupied with their own interests at the expense of the couple or family. But discouraging your spouse from getting together with his or her friends can leave an emptiness and lack of support in their lives. Trying to reconnect with these people and interests is often harder with time away. Some move on and find new friends and activities and lose touch altogether. Being able to share and compare what is going on in each of your lives helps provide a sounding-board, a place to vent and provide support that is missing when you have no one else. It is a release away from the stresses and strains of life, often where there is unconditional support and caring.

Back to our empty-nesters…hopefully, they've supported each other to maintain and nurture friendships and outside interests, while still making and taking time to enjoy time together as a couple. Hopefully, they've talked about their future together when the children have grown, are closer to achieving the goals and dreams they had planned together years before. Now, they have the greater freedom of more time to enjoy them. Closer to retirement or ready to retire, the pressures and stresses of work may be less or more if they've seen savings drained away with paying for education or the economy. Some of us may have to work longer, some may take early retirement. The focus changes again to their future together…whether to down-size where they live away from the big family house to something perhaps cheaper and more manageable, perhaps planning those vacations they had dreamed of together for years.

Of course, there will always be the children, grown up and on their own now, creating their own futures, careers, marriages and families. You will always be a part of their lives. Hopefully, the closeness and caring becomes a burgeoning, supportive friendship as you can still provide the guidance and wealth of life experience they seek out. As they enter the work-world, into relationships, marriages and being parents themselves, they can now recognize and appreciate all that you have to give.

You have earned your time together now as a couple, having weathered the storm of being parents. You've worked hard together to make a home and a family together, what a tremendous accomplishment! Now is your time to be a couple again together, two people who have grown and changed over time. Reflect on the changes in each other over the years and marvel at the people you've become. The experiences you've been through have only served to strengthen you, to be able to trust each other even more, to support each other through everything. You have truly lived every bit of your marriage vows through everything. Remember that and celebrate…and keep on growing!!!

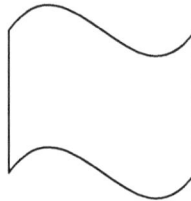